A PLACE
AT THE TABLE

A PLACE — AT THE TABLE

FRESH RECIPES
for meaningful gatherings

Kelly Minter

with REGINA PINTO

B&H PUBLISHING
NASHVILLE, TENNESSEE

KELLY MINTER is passionate about teaching the Bible, and believes it permeates all of life. When she's not writing, speaking, or singing you can find her picking homegrown vegetables, cooking meals, enjoying her six nieces and nephews or riding a boat down the Amazon River with Justice & Mercy International. A Southern transplant, she delights in college football, neighborhood walks, and a diner mug of good coffee with her closest friends.

REGINA PINTO A self-taught chef who learned the basics of cooking from her grandmother and mother in Brazil, Regina has traveled through the US and UK, merging the flavors of her childhood with each new destination. She is a chocolatier and pastry chef, and the former owner of the Blushing Berry in Tennessee, where she created truffles and desserts for some of Nashville's most famous brands, including Arrington Vineyards, Belle Meade, and the Hermitage Hotel. She thinks of cooking as a way to express her love for others and finds the greatest joy in seeing people delight in her dishes, especially her family, as she is the mother of two and grandmother of three. Regina is a member of Rolling Hills Community Church in Franklin, Tennessee, and is active with Justice and Mercy International in the Amazon.

*To Mom and Dad,
for always giving us
a place at the table.*

CONTENTS

— THE NEW CHURCH POTLUCK —

— IN DEFENSE OF SOUP —

— A BIG FISH STORY FROM THE AMAZON —

— BREAKFAST AND THE ART OF INVITATION —

— SPECIAL OCCASIONS —

— SWEET CELEBRATIONS —

WHY COOKING
MATTERS

———

My love for food and cooking was cultivated by growing up in a family that loved to eat and a home where my mom made dinner most evenings. These early experiences at home also helped set the table for my love of people and conversation—for the simple reason that food and meaningful gatherings feed one another. And this isn't just a pun talking. A conversation is always better with a cup of coffee and muffin in hand, and a cup of coffee and a muffin is undoubtedly more sublime with a person to share them with.

When we make the time to cook a meal, we're much more likely to take the time to savor it with others. When we slow down long enough for our palettes to discern seasonal flavors, experiment with a new ingredient, or grow a vegetable in our garden, we learn to appreciate God's remarkable creation and the journey it makes into our kitchens and on to our plates. And when the meals we make are shared with others at the table, I like to think that this is when a dish is at its best—when it can look around the room and say to itself, *I have arrived!*

The difficulty, of course, is that we live in a busy and hurried society that leaves us little time for cooking, especially with quality ingredients that taste good. That's why, with a little bit of planning, the recipes in this cookbook are accessible and doable. (We did include a few slightly more challenging ones for those who have the time to experiment, compliments of Regina.) The goal is not to burden you, but to empower you to cherish even the simplest meals with loved ones. Because when we don't make the time for cooking, good food isn't the only casualty. We miss out on all the conversations and laughter that naturally happen in a busy kitchen and around a table of homemade food.

Whenever cooking feels like a debilitating chore for me, or that I don't have the time for it, I'm reminded of an afternoon when I was in the Amazon jungle and a native pastor's wife, Maria, welcomed me into her home. She was serving chicken for dinner and asked me to stay. What I didn't realize at the time was that said chicken was in the backyard. Alive. Tottering around the grounds, blissfully unaware that this dear and gracious woman, filled with the Holy Spirit, was about to snap its head off. Maria's care of this bird from birth to, well, chicken soup, was a far cry from me having to run to the refrigerated aisle of the grocery store for two boneless, skinless breasts. Perspective.

Food is a blessing and cooking is an invitation for us to be involved in that blessing. When we cook, we're more grateful for God's gift of food.

While many of us will never have to cultivate our food, harvest it, cook it, and finally eat it for survival like Maria did, my hope is that we'll at least hang onto the cooking piece. Why? Because what I simply cannot get away from, what has changed me over the years, is that food is a blessing and cooking is an invitation for us to be involved in that blessing. When we cook, we're more grateful for God's gift of food, we're more connected to the miracle of His creation, and we're reflecting His creativity. And on top of all of those reasons—cooking is better for us and better for those around us. After all, sharing the meals we make with others is one of life's greatest joys. At least I think so.

Whether you're a novice or a pro in the kitchen, or somewhere in between, my prayer is that this collection of recipes and stories will inspire and empower you to nourish others and yourself. To sniff a new spice or try a new culinary technique. To invite a guest to your table, and perhaps introduce them to the God who made all the flavors and people they are enjoying.

In the fast-paced culture we live in, cooking matters because it's one of the last connections we have left to our food besides eating it. And in our often lonely society, cooking is one of the last connections we have to each other. My hope is that *A Place at the Table* will support and encourage you to reclaim some space in your life and home for this good and meaningful endeavor. ❧

THE FOOD
THAT BRINGS
US TOGETHER

I can't pinpoint when my love for cooking boiled over, but it has been simmering since my growing-up years around the family dinner table.

Our family has always loved food. We were the ones who would discuss what we wanted for our afternoon snack over breakfast. Meals were the perfect time to talk about subsequent meals. Our family dinners weren't fancy, but they were consistent—something I could count on no matter what took place that day at school, or at basketball practice, or more tenuously in my often-anxious brain. Our family meals served as more than nourishment for our bodies; the dinner table was a mooring where we could always find safe harbor.

It was here at the family table where I began to appreciate food and the community it inevitably brings. We ate and we talked. We ate and we laughed. We ate and we fought over who got to sit in what seat, complaining about the minced onions in the meatloaf that my mom snuck in even when I begged her not to.

"Mom!" I'd slump over my plate, "I hate onions."

"Kelly, you can't even taste them, they're so small."

"Well if you can't taste them, then why do you put them in there?"

Then my dad would get involved and talk to me about my problem with sassiness. The minced onions in the meatloaf were a whole thing, which is why there is no meatloaf recipe in this cookbook. In general, I still have a hard time with the word *minced*.

Our family found out a lot about one another while eating together. Sometimes information we didn't always want to know. Once when my brother, David, was around six years old, it was his turn to pray over the meal. We all held hands as he thanked God for something he appreciated in particular about each of us, the way his Sunday school teacher prayed over her class.

"Dear God," he earnestly opened, "Thank You for Dad, who we love so much and who always plays with us."

He squinted his eyes to see who was sitting next to Dad, then clenched them tight again. "And for Megan, who is always so nice to me and shares with me. And thank You for Katie, who plays games with me. And thank You for Mom, for taking me to school and buying me stuff."

I was last in the circle. "And thank You for Kelly, who . . ." after a minor pause, "actually, I don't really like Kelly that much."

It was a shocking moment of honesty. My sisters erupted into roars of laughter while my parents tried to conceal their amusement so as not to embarrass my brother. David's praying eyelids split open, genuinely wondering what was so funny. Prayers were supposed to be earnest, right? I don't remember the specifics of why David was upset with me in that moment, other than the fact that I was the big sister in high school and he was probably in my superior way. I've spent the better part of my adult life trying to make up for this most unfortunate season in our relationship. We haven't explicitly spoken about this, but it's understood that I owe him chips and guacamole for the rest of his life.

I'm forever grateful to my parents and their determination to solidify family dinners as part of our daily routines. I realize that times continue to change and not everyone can prepare meals every single day of the week, but my mom's regular habit of cooking and calling us to the table fostered stability and community in our family and gave us grounding that I'm not sure we would have found elsewhere.

Without even realizing it, we were learning attributes about Jesus as my parents not only served and fed us, but also modeled grace, kindness, and even friendship.

The dinner table was a place where we could ask questions. Inevitably situations arose from our day for which we needed wisdom: What does it look like to show humility when you win in sports? How should you embody graciousness when you don't get the solo in choir? How do you respond to the person at school who's been unkind? What does having character mean and why is it important? The dinner table wasn't just a place for us to share our own stories; it was also a place where we were taught to think about the needs of others. Along with thanking God for our meal, we'd often pray for people we knew were hurting and then through conversation we kids would hear about the ways our parents were helping in those situations. All of those things and more were shared together while eating together. In the subtlest of ways our meal times nourished our souls as much as our bodies.

Our family meals served as more than nourishment for our bodies; the dinner table was a mooring where we could always find safe habor.

I'm thankful for my dad's role in our family meals too. While my dad is not a cook per se, he added to the food milieu of our household in his own, very unique, ways. He didn't really make meals for us as much as he would get on certain culinary kicks. Like the time he decided that our store-bought bread was as nutritious as cardboard, and bought a professional-grade blender to grind his own wheat berries.

"Mike, I wouldn't know a wheat berry if it hit me in the head," my Mom lamented. "Can't you just be normal and go buy wheat flour at the grocery store like everyone else?"

The answers to these reasonable questions were "no" and "no."

A few days later, in waltzed my dad dragging six behemoth bags of wheat berries into our laundry room, some of them appearing to contain dead bodies. The wheat berries weren't hitting us in the head, but we were tripping over the burlap sacks they were stored in while trying to do laundry. I don't remember my parents fighting over much, but the bread-making kick with its blenders, cooking utensils that cluttered the countertops, loaf pans, and body bags of wheat was cause for strife. Unlike my mom who didn't overthink the meals she prepared, everything my dad made had to be pulled from the ground or plucked from a tree.

Dad's commitment to natural foods ended up creating a few annual traditions. For example, every October we had four thousand pounds of homemade applesauce as a result of him leading the six of us on apple-picking outings to Stribling Orchard. In the summers, we always had a few slicing tomatoes, squash, and zucchini he grew from his modest garden. And then there were the occasional times of year he decided to make bread (which felt like a several-day affair), and we got to enjoy special toast for breakfast. While his food contributions were delicious, they came to us in fits and spurts—we would have starved under his purist ways.

My mom's consistent example of practical and efficient cooking combined with my dad's fascination for what can be grown and prepared straight from the ground has given me an appreciation for both. On busy nights when I can only find the time to use the ingredients I have on hand, I can tap into my mom's strengths and swiftly throw a pasta dish together, pairing it with a simple salad. On other nights when I have more time, I'll channel my dad, making something like homemade salsa verde with the bowl of fresh tomatillos that are sitting on my kitchen counter, recently picked straight from my garden. This takes a little more time, of course, especially when you think of how long it takes to grow a tomatillo.

Did you know that tomatillo plants have to grow in pairs so they can cross-pollinate? I didn't find this out until after planting a single one in my garden, which apparently would not do. If I were going to be able to make my own zesty salsa verde, I would have to quickly plant another tomatillo plant next to the original.

Fortunately I had plans to take Will and Harper (my nephew and niece) to the park and could deftly swing by the farmer's market on the way—how could I pass up using my newfound gardening knowledge as a teaching opportunity?

"Why didn't you get your plant before picking us up?" they wailed, while I marched them through aisle after aisle of plants.

See, they didn't understand my dad's ways that have now become my ways, which is essentially this: the more complicated and time consuming, the better.

But the trip to the market yielded a wonderful result: the kids can now identify a tomatillo plant out of a line of vegetable suspects. And they love dipping excessive amounts of chips into bowls of my homemade salsa verde. That one trip, along with many years of eating chips and dip, has created an experience together that they'll appreciate in approximately thirty years. Experiences my parents created for me and my siblings.

As a child I didn't grasp the heart, heritage, or sheer labor that lay behind every one of my mom's casseroles or my dad's wheat bread. We were just happy to be gathered together over our favorite foods. Which is the point, I think. The difference now as adults is that if we want these wonderful meals and depth of relationships, *we* have to do the cooking for them. We can't just pull up a chair like we used to and complain about the onions.

My prayer is that family members, friends, and even strangers will find not only safe harbor around your table, but also the attributes of Christ Himself.

Perhaps these are all the reasons I wanted to write a cookbook. Not because I'm a seasoned chef (Regina Pinto to the rescue), but because of the shared experiences, rich conversations, and deepening of relationships that happen so naturally around cooking and eating. These warm memories of nourishment and togetherness at my childhood family table have cultivated a desire in me to gather others in the same way, where together, we can savor community through cooking. Offering a meaningful gathering and a seat at the table has become the entire purview of this collection of stories and recipes that you hold in your hands.

If you are aiming to bring community together over meals that require little more than some time, along with whole and accessible ingredients, I offer you *A Place at the Table*. By arming you with some recipes and encouragement, my prayer is that family members, friends, and even strangers will find not only safe harbor around your table, but also the attributes of Christ Himself. Wheat berries not required. ❧

Simple Salad
(recipe on p. 15)

12

Homemade Pizza
(recipe on p. 14)

HOMEMADE PIZZA

PREP TIME: 20 minutes (plus 1 hour for rising) | **COOK TIME:** 40 minutes | **MAKES:** 2–3 small pizzas

CRUST

1 ½ cups water

1 package dry yeast

7 tablespoons olive oil

1 ½ teaspoons salt

1 teaspoon sugar

4 cups flour, divided

PIZZA SAUCE

1 (28 ounce) can San Marzano tomatoes, draining optional

1 tablespoon olive oil

2 teaspoons salt

½ teaspoon oregano

Optional: Red pepper flakes

INGREDIENT IDEAS FOR TOPPING

Asiago cheese, arugula, prosciutto, olive oil, salt, pepper

Pesto, Ricotta cheese, spinach, basil leaves, mushrooms, olive oil

Tomato sauce, shredded mozzarella, oregano, olive oil

Caesar salad with Parmesan cheese shavings

Fontina cheese, figs, balsamic vinegar

Tomato sauce, Mozzarella cheese, green bell peppers, sausage, olives, mushrooms, onions

Ricotta cheese, caramelized onions, prosciutto, Gruyère cheese

1. **TO MAKE CRUST:** In a large bowl, dissolve yeast in warm water. Add 3 tablespoons of olive oil, 1 1/2 teaspoons of salt, and 1 teaspoon of sugar. Stir to combine.

2. Add 2 cups of flour. Beat with an electric mixer or wooden spoon. Then add the remaining 2 cups of flour, one at a time, mixing as you go.

3. Knead until smooth, about 5 minutes. Place dough in a bowl greased with olive oil, brush the top of the dough with olive oil, and cover with a damp cloth. Place in a warm location for about 1 hour. (I warm the oven just a little, and then turn it off and place bowl in oven.)

4. After the dough rises, take it out of the oven (or warm location) and punch it down (push your fists gently and firmly into the middle of the dough). Then wrap the edges of the dough into its center, creating a ball.

5. Sprinkle the countertop with flour, take the dough out of the bowl, and lightly roll it out. After you are finished rolling it, place dough into lightly greased pizza pan. Brush dough with the remaining olive oil, if desired. Let it rise again for 1 hour. (You can omit this step if you are short on time.)

6. Preheat oven to 400 degrees.

7. Once dough has risen to your satisfaction, cover with sauce and your favorite pizza toppings (see ingredients list) and bake until dough is golden-brown and toppings are cooked through.

8. **TO MAKE SAUCE:** Put the tomatoes (and juice if desired) and all spices in the blender and pulse 3–4 times to a smooth consistency. Do not over-pulse.

PIZZA ADAPTATIONS

With the same dough, you can make a calzone, an Italian folded pizza usually filled with Ricotta cheese, Mozzarella cheese, small pieces of ham or prosciutto, and tomato sauce. After folding and pressing to seal the edges, brush with tomato sauce, sprinkle with Parmesan cheese, and bake.

You can also create a tomato Sicilian pizza that looks so beautiful. Spray a 9 x 13-inch pan, roll the dough on the pan and let it rise for 1 hour until it doubles in size. Peel tomatoes and cut them in half like a basket and remove seeds. Arrange the tomatoes on the dough side by side. Then, in each basket add some chopped garlic and a little piece of alici (anchovies). Finish by drizzling with olive oil and salt, and bake until golden. Alici is optional.

SIMPLE SALAD

PREP TIME: 10 minutes | **COOK TIME:** 0 minutes | **Serves:** 6

SALAD

2 heads of red leaf lettuce, washed

½ red onion, sliced thin

1 cucumber, sliced thin

1 cup cherry tomatoes, sliced in half

DRESSING

2 tablespoons olive oil

1 tablespoon red wine vinegar or lemon juice

Salt and pepper, to taste

½ teaspoon Dijon mustard

1. Toss all salad ingredients in a large bowl.
2. In a separate bowl, mix all dressing ingredients together.
3. Drizzle the dressing mixture on the salad.

Pizza is one of my favorite meals to make because it's a community affair. My brother makes the homemade dough and the sauce, the rest of us bring the toppings and throw together a simple salad to go with it. Having a salad always makes me feel healthier about eating pizza.

K

Pictured on page 12 ❖

SUN-DRIED TOMATO BOW TIE PASTA

PREP TIME: 30 minutes | **COOK TIME:** 20 minutes | **SERVES:** 4–6

2 packages sun-dried tomatoes, softened and cut in strips

16 ounces bow tie pasta

2–3 tablespoons olive oil

10 cloves garlic, minced

½ cup pine nuts

16 ounces Feta cheese, crumbled

1 (16 ounce) can black olives, chopped

Salt and pepper, to taste

Optional: 1 pound boneless, skinless chicken breast, cut into small pieces

1. Soften the sun-dried tomatoes according to the package directions and cut in strips.
2. Cook pasta according to package directions. Drain pasta; set aside.
3. While the pasta cooks, if you are adding chicken to this recipe, cut chicken into bite-size pieces and set aside.
4. Heat olive oil over medium heat in a sauté pan. When the oil is warm, add garlic and sauté for 2 minutes. Add sun-dried tomatoes and sauté for another 2–3 minutes.
5. If using optional chicken, add the chicken to the sauté pan and cook until done. Add chicken and sun-dried tomato mixture to the pasta, sprinkle with pine nuts, Feta cheese, and olives. Serve immediately.

I've been making this pasta dish for years. Whether just for myself or for my friends, this is one of my favorite recipes because of how easy it is to make while being uniquely delicious. I chalk this up to the sun-dried tomatoes and pine nuts.

Cilantro Black Beans with Salsa, Avocado, and Rice (recipe on p. 20)

Cilantro Chicken
Enchiladas
(recipe on p. 21)

CILANTRO BLACK BEANS WITH SALSA, AVOCADO, AND RICE

PREP TIME: 30 minutes | **COOK TIME:** 1 hour 20 minutes | **SERVES:** 6–8

4 cans (15 ounces each) black beans, undrained

2 cups brown rice

½ yellow onion, chopped

1 bunch fresh cilantro

6 cloves garlic, minced

1 tablespoon olive oil

12 ounces shredded Monterey Jack cheese, divided

2 avocados, peeled, pitted, and sliced

1 jar salsa

1 cup sour cream

Bag of tortilla chips

1. Heat black beans in a saucepan over medium heat, keeping most of the sauce from the cans. (Allow beans to warm for 20 minutes.)
2. In a separate pot, prepare brown rice according to package instructions. Set aside.
3. Chop onion and cilantro, and mince the garlic. Warm olive oil in a sauté pan over medium heat, approximately 1 minute. Sauté onion, cilantro, and garlic in olive oil.
4. Preheat oven to 325 degrees.
5. Stir the onion mixture into the black beans.
6. Pour black bean mixture into a 9 x 13-inch pan, and top with 8 ounces of the shredded Monterey Jack cheese, covering extensively. Cover with aluminum foil and bake for 30 minutes.
7. Serve black bean mixture over rice alongside a nice spread of avocado slices, salsa, sour cream, tortilla chips, and the remaining shredded cheese for a beautiful presentation.

K

If you like cilantro this will be your new favorite. It's a simple, hearty, and inexpensive dish, but don't let that make you think it's short on flavor. I've served this more times than I can count and my friends and family always ask me for the recipe.

CILANTRO CHICKEN ENCHILADAS

PREP TIME: 45 minutes | **COOK TIME:** 20–30 minutes | **SERVES:** 6–8

6 boneless, skinless chicken breasts, shredded (reserve 2 cups of broth)

1 teaspoon cumin

½ cup tightly packed fresh cilantro

½ cup sour cream

2 cups canned chicken broth

8 burrito-sized tortillas

8 tablespoons salsa, medium or hot

Optional: 2 cans black beans, rinsed and drained

4 ounces Monterey Jack cheese, grated

4 ounces Cheddar cheese, grated

GRAVY

½ stick butter

1 tablespoon flour

1. Preheat oven to 350 degrees. Boil chicken breasts for 20 minutes and reserve 2 cups of leftover broth when draining. Shred the chicken breasts.

2. **TO MAKE GRAVY:** In a blender, mix cumin, cilantro, sour cream, 1 cup canned chicken broth, and 1 cup reserved chicken broth.

3. In a skillet or saucepan, heat butter slowly and add flour until smooth. Slowly add 2 remaining cups of chicken broth until smooth and creamy. (If a thicker consistency is desired, add more flour.) Add this mixture to the contents of the blender, and blend together.

4. **TO MAKE ENCHILADAS:** Fill each tortilla with 1/3 cup shredded chicken and 1–2 tablespoons of salsa. Add some of the optional black beans if desired. Roll tortillas and place in a 9 x 13-inch pan, seam-side down.

5. Fill pan with gravy from blender, completely covering the enchiladas. Sprinkle cheeses on top. Bake uncovered for 30 minutes.

This is perhaps one of my all-time favorite dishes. Your friends will love you for taking the time to tackle this one. (And it's even better the next day.)

K

Pictured on page 19 ❖

THE BENEFITS OF CANNING

We all wish we could somehow bottle the freshness and flavors of summertime fruits and vegetables so we can enjoy them throughout the year. In many ways, canning makes this possible. If you've never canned before, it's like bottling the flavors of August so you can crack them open in the bleak of January. It's storing July tomatoes so you can pour them into February sauces. It's capturing June raspberries so you can spread them onto March's toast. Do you see the genius here? Canning allows you to savor some of summer's signature flavors year-round, which is a real benefit when Daylight Savings ends, it's freezing outside, and the sun sets at 4:00 in the afternoon— this is how it works in Nashville, anyway. Believe me, nothing will cheer your spirits in the dead of winter like opening a jar of fig preserves you canned yourself and spreading the goodness onto a cracker with a smear of Brie cheese.

It's storing July tomatoes so you can pour them into February sauces. It's capturing June raspberries so you can spread them onto March's toast.

I'll admit that canning is a bit of work. Boiling the jars, measuring your ingredients, blanching, skinning, cutting out bruised spots, wiping the rims before screwing on the tops just so. It can be a messy and time-consuming affair, and you typically have to have a lot of whatever it is you're canning on hand to make it worth it. Also, if you've never used a pressure canner there's the real threat of the lid blowing a hole through your roof, possibly hitting a low-hanging planet. I still have a healthy fear of my pressure canner, although in reality there's not much to worry about. You just have to practice with it. Have I sold you? The upside is that canning can be a lot of fun if you do it with friends or family, and even cathartic if you do it by yourself.

While many of us can today for the pure joy of savoring the flavors of summer, our ancestors canned out of necessity to sustain them through the leanness of winter. Many people still can their food for this reason. The process of canning helps me appreciate what life used to be like—and still is—for so many.

It gives me a greater appreciation for the food we enjoy and reminds me that preservation is a blessing. As soon as my nieces and nephews are old enough, I'm hoping to get them in on a day of canning. I'll let you know how that goes.

Canning also makes for great gifts. My friend Rachel's parents have a farm in Georgia, and every year they send her home with a few jars of produce to give to me that they've canned from their crops. I'm never so happy than when someone gives me a jar of Roma tomatoes, salsa, pickles, raspberry jam, or a starter jar of vegetable soup. What better gift than the one that's edible? Or the one that someone has poured her time and labor into?

To get started, you can educate yourself in so many different ways: purchase an inexpensive book on canning, search the Internet, look for instructions on the packages of canning supplies, ask a family member to teach you, or join a local community class. Just be careful that your canning recipes come from a trusted source and you follow directions closely. Bacteria can be a real threat, but shouldn't be an issue if you follow the prescribed steps. You won't need a lot of equipment to can, but you will need a few pieces. Once you make a minimal investment, you'll have most of what you need for the long haul. If you are wondering what type of produce to start with, I would start with the tomato. But that should come as no surprise. ❖

ROASTED CHICKEN WITH ROOT VEGETABLES

PREP TIME: 30 minutes | **COOK TIME:** 45 minutes–1 hour | **SERVES:** 8

SPICE RUB

Salt and pepper, to taste

½ teaspoon onion powder

½ teaspoon garlic powder

½ teaspoon paprika

1 teaspoon sage, chopped

10 fresh sprigs thyme

5 tablespoons butter, room temperature

MEAT

1 large roasting chicken, whole or cut in half

VEGETABLES

5 mini new potatoes, cut in half

2 sweet potatoes, cubed

4 red potatoes, cubed

1 small butternut squash, cubed

2 medium carrots, sliced

1 cup pearl onions

8 cloves garlic

4 tablespoons olive oil

Salt and pepper, to taste

1. Preheat oven to 350 degrees.
2. Make the spice rub with salt and pepper, to taste, onion powder, garlic powder, paprika, sage, sprigs of thyme, and butter, mixing well. Rub the chicken with the spice mixture and set aside.
3. Mix the vegetables with olive oil, and salt and pepper, to taste. Spread the vegetables around the bottom of a roasting pan.
4. Drop the chicken on top of the vegetables and bake for 45 minutes (if the chicken is in halves) to 1 hour (if the chicken is whole), or until chicken is done and golden in color.

What could possibly be exciting about chicken, you ask? To which I respond, a whole chicken properly roasted is still one of my favorite meals to eat. A whole chicken has a flavor you don't get from the boneless/skinless fare. Try this with seasonal vegetables and you'll remember what's so great about chicken.

MK's Taco Salad
(recipe on p. 28)

Big Fat Greek Salad
with Grilled Chicken
(recipe on p. 29)

MK'S TACO SALAD

PREP TIME: 30 minutes | **COOK TIME:** 9–12 minutes | **SERVES:** 8

MEAT

1 pound ground beef

1 tablespoon chili powder

1 teaspoon ground cumin

½ teaspoon onion powder

½ teaspoon garlic powder

¼ teaspoon dried oregano

¼ teaspoon paprika

¼ teaspoon ground coriander

1 tablespoon olive oil

Salt and pepper, to taste

SALAD

1 head romaine or red leaf lettuce, chopped

1 cup tomatoes, chopped

1 cucumber, chopped

2 tablespoons green onion, chopped

2 tablespoons cilantro, chopped

1 (15 ounce) can black or pinto beans, rinsed and drained

1 cup Mexican cheese, shredded

Optional: 1 pickled jalapeño

1 avocado, peeled, pitted, and sliced

DRESSING AND SIDES

½ cup sour cream

1 cup salsa

Bag of tortilla chips

1. Combine the ground beef with chili powder, ground cumin, onion powder, garlic powder, dried oregano, paprika, and ground coriander, mixing with your hands until well combined.

2. In a large skillet over medium-high heat, heat the olive oil. Add the ground beef and fry, breaking up the meat using a wooden spoon. Stir constantly as the meat cooks, until the beef is completely browned, 9–12 minutes. Keep warm.

3. In a large salad bowl, add lettuce, tomato, cucumber, green onion, cilantro, beans, Mexican cheese, and optional pickled jalapeño. Toss to combine.

4. Add the ground beef to the salad mixture and toss again. Add the pieces of avocado on top.

5. In a small bowl, mix the sour cream and salsa and drizzle over salad. Serve with tortilla chips.

❖ *Pictured on page 26*

BIG FAT GREEK SALAD WITH GRILLED CHICKEN

PREP TIME: 30 minutes–1 hour | **COOK TIME:** 25–30 minutes | **SERVES:** 6–8

MARINADE

2 tablespoons olive oil

1 handful fresh oregano (dry oregano can be substituted if needed)

Juice from half a lemon

Salt and pepper, to taste

¼ cup water

MEAT

2 boneless, skinless chicken breasts (bone-in breast works great also)

DRESSING

4 tablespoons olive oil

Juice from 1 lemon (add more to make it zestier)

2 tablespoons water

1 tablespoon Greek seasoning

Freshly ground black pepper, to taste

SALAD

2 heads Romaine lettuce, chopped

1 cup Hearts of palm, chopped

1 cup Artichoke hearts, chopped

½ cup Sun-dried tomatoes, chopped

½ cup Feta cheese

Optional: ½ cup toasted pine nuts

OPTIONAL SIDES

Warm pita bread

Tzatziki sauce

1. Combine all marinade ingredients and pour into a zipped bag. Place chicken in the bag and marinate in refrigerator for 30 minutes to 1 hour.
2. While the chicken marinates, mix the Greek dressing ingredients together in a small bowl and set aside. Prepare the chopped ingredients for the salad.
3. Place lettuce in a large salad bowl and arrange other salad ingredients on top.
4. Grill the chicken breasts on an outdoor grill for 25–30 minutes or until done. Slice chicken into strips.
5. Toss salad with Greek dressing and then serve with chicken.
6. Optional: Serve with warm pita bread and tzatziki sauce.

I really love this when I need something healthy but don't want to feel like I'm eating healthy. The Feta cheese, artichoke hearts, and sun-dried tomatoes burst with flavor. And the grilled chicken, especially if you can grill it on the bone, turns the salad into a satisfying meal.

K

Pictured on page 27 ❖

FRESH FROM
THE GARDEN

M ost of us live in environments where we consider the source of our food as being synonymous with the grocery store instead of from where it actually comes. When my niece Maryn was five, I took her to the supermarket to pick up a gallon of milk.

I slid the carton off the shelf and casually mentioned, "Can you believe this comes from cows?" (These are my aunt attempts at being educational.) She furrowed her brows and looked at me like I'd just told her that our dairy products come from the tooth fairy.

"Cows?" she grimaced. "Milk comes from the grocery store, silly!"

In addition to losing all faith in our educational system, I realized that for much of my life I had also been fairly ignorant about the birthplace of most of the fresh produce I regularly buy and eat. By the time a cluster of grapes, sweet onion, or Roma tomato got to me, they had been picked from a tree, pulled from the ground, or twisted from a vine, leaving me little idea of how they grew, much less where or when they grew.

Do asparaguses dangle from trees? (They don't.)

Do potatoes have green, leafy stalks above the ground? (They do.)

Does a squash emerge from orange flowers that are also edible? (Yes and yes.)

Are Brussels sprouts . . .

a) individual vegetables harvested from beneath the soil or

b) found congregating around a thick stalk that towers two feet above the ground?

(Answer b.)

Why is the word *Brussels* in their name? (I have no idea.)

The question is: Does any of this really matter? As long as we can get whatever fruits and vegetables we want at the store, do we need to know how they grow, when they grow, or where they come from? I suppose the answer depends on what your goal is when it comes to food.

I remember the first year I grew sugar snap peas in my garden. I planted them in the bleak chill of February, impressed by their willingness to pierce through the soil as though winter was no match for their sturdy shoots—gardening is nothing if not one spiritual metaphor after another. By April, their smooth vines had twisted around my trellises, now dripping with plump pods dotted with delicate white blooms at their tips. I picked a basket's worth and tossed them into a bowl for my friends Belle and Kathy to try. You can enjoy the whole pod or pull its tip like a loose thread all the way down its seam and pluck the peas out individually. No matter how you eat them, these little green pearls are a springtime marvel when enjoyed fresh. While Kathy popped peas into her mouth she turned to Belle, "Do you grow your own food like this?"

"No," Belle said, "I just go to the grocery store."

Gardening allows me to move about in the great outdoors; it's the perfect place for my mind to bounce between thoughts while watching a bee alight from one tomato flower to the other.

Fair enough. Given our fast-paced society that thrives on convenience, quantity, immediacy, and global variety, going to the grocery store is by far the most pragmatic and time-efficient option. The backyard garden meets hardly any of these demands. In fact, the only quick thing a garden offers is weeds. (Or the zucchini you decided to leave on the vine for one more day that overnight turned into a baseball bat.) But I didn't start my hobby of gardening for expediency.

For one thing, the art of cultivating something is an absolute joy for me. Maybe this is due to my work of studying, reading, and writing that requires me to sit still and think deeply for long periods of time. Gardening allows me to move about in the great outdoors; it's the perfect place for my mind to bounce between thoughts while watching a bee alight from one tomato flower to the other. Unlike so much of the writing I do, where effectiveness is sometimes hard to measure and gratification is delayed by years, I can weed a garden bed in thirty minutes and see the fruit of my labor: a clean rectangle of soil growing only the plants I want growing there. See how nicely this also plays into my desire to control things? (Note: Nothing will shatter your illusion of control like blight, aphids, lettuce nibbling rabbits, or the perfectly evil tomato hornworm.)

In addition to the cathartic nature of tending my garden, cultivating has been a peaceful activity for me. I can be given to worry and anxiousness if I'm not careful. The Internet with its string of bad news and the phone with its continual alerts and distractions feed this tendency in me. When I'm in the garden I can leave it all behind, and not out of pure denial or blissful ignorance. Surrounded by plants that peacefully bear their fruit in season, I'm reminded of Jesus' words to abide in Him as a branch abides in the vine (John 15). And when I clip the stem of a zinnia or lacecap hydrangea, I think of His comforting exhortation in Matthew 6:27–34. In the garden, I have the time to wonder: How might His words sound today if He were walking with me through the great outdoors?

What do you think your worry will accomplish? Look with me for a moment and ponder this flower. Have you ever seen it exhaustedly spinning thread in a nervous frenzy to clothe itself? Not even Hollywood's most beautiful or Forbes' *wealthiest is clothed in the glory of this knockout rose, or this tulip ushering in spring. If your Father in heaven is this good to the temporary, soul-less flower, how much more will he take care of you? Oh you of tiny faith.*

You don't really get this experience walking through the aisles of the grocery store.

How might His words sound today if He were walking with me through my garden?

Among the many reasons I planted a garden—in addition to its spiritual reminders and therapeutic offerings—is the simple reward of flavor. We're so used to getting whatever vegetable or ingredient we want, from wherever we want, when we want—regardless of whether it's in season—that we've forgotten what *fresh* tastes like. What *seasonal* looks like. And maybe even what *waiting* and *anticipation* feel like. Looking forward to certain fruits and vegetables emerging in certain seasons creates anticipation, seasonally specific memories, and gratitude for special occasions.

Farm-to-table restaurants have made popular an ancient principle: produce in its season tastes better. So here's my secret to dinner parties and cooking in general: do your best to serve what's in season. These have become trendy terms, yes, but forget about trends for a moment—this is about taste and timeliness.

In the fall, try your hand at the butternut squash and sausage risotto. In the winter, make a turkey vegetable soup with rice. When the milder temperatures of spring arrive, cook with cruciferous vegetables like cauliflower, Brussels sprouts, and broccoli. Or serve English garden peas over pasta with a side of glazed carrots. When summer hits, get your hands on every fresh vegetable your region grows and roast it, steam it, bake it, grill it, sauté it, or eat it raw. And by all means, pull seasonal fruits into your desserts.

I remember a dinner party I threw for a group of girls who were part of my Cultivate events. I'd thought so much about the dinner I was making that I'd forgotten about dessert. On the way home from the store I passed a peach truck, bought a paper bag's worth, chopped them, tossed them into individual ice cream bowls, topped them with homemade whipped cream, added a sprig of mint, and served them after dinner. It was the easiest thing in the world and still my friends were looking at me like *how do you do it?* If I could take the slightest bit of credit for the invention of the peach tree, I would. But the real secret was the simple fact that these peaches were in season. How novel of them.

It should be strongly noted here that you don't have to grow your own garden to cook seasonally. I'm dependent upon the grocery store as much as anyone. But most of us can visit a nearby farmer's market to peruse its seasonal offerings. You can also join Community Supported Agriculture (CSA) that delivers boxes of weekly harvests to a local spot in your community. Or simply go to the grocery store and look for the sections of local or regional produce, and pay attention to what is generally in season.

I don't come close to adhering to these principals all the time—they are easier to implement in certain months compared to others. Obviously winter can be trying unless you've canned in the summer (see pages 22–23). Or if you live in a place like Maui, in which case you don't need any cooking help because life is perfect for you. Cooking seasonally is mostly about paying attention to what month you're in, and what grows at that time in your area. Your dinner guests will appreciate the difference between fresh versus what's been flown in from Zanzibar. They'll shower you with praise, and all the while you'll know it was the fresh fruits and vegetables that did all the heavy lifting. It's the secret of combining seasonal and local to create astonishingly flavorful.

We know from Scripture that every season is a perennial reminder of God's faithfulness as long as our world remains.

As I've grown older, seasonal foods have become more meaningful to me, partially because of the seasons they represent. The author of Ecclesiastes put it this way: "There is a time for everything, and a season for every activity under the heavens . . . a time to plant and a time to uproot" (3:1–2 NIV). Even difficult seasons are part of God's plan for our lives, and we can take comfort in knowing that no season lasts forever. Each one tells of God's goodness to us, whether the first buds of spring are emerging plump with the promise of new life, or the glory of the autumn leaf is drifting to the ground in colorful flame. We know from Scripture that every season is a perennial reminder of God's faithfulness as long as our world remains. "As long as the earth endures, seedtime and harvest, cold and heat, summer and winter, and day and night will not cease" (Gen. 8:22).

As I think about what I want my young nieces and nephews to remember about the dinners they eat at my table (besides hotdogs and frozen pizza), and what I want my friends and guests to remember, it's the creative, timely, and nourishing care of our Creator. The March asparagus, May strawberry, June garlic scape, October squash, January canned tomatoes—each of them tell a story of God's provision punctuated by flavor and stamped by a season. "He has made everything beautiful in its time" (Eccles. 3:11 NIV). ❧

SUMMER CHERRY TOMATO AND BASIL PASTA

PREP TIME: 15 minutes | **COOK TIME:** 30 minutes | **SERVES:** 4–6

1 (12 ounce) package linguini pasta

Cherry tomatoes (1 pint), sliced in half (whole tomatoes, chopped will also work)

5 cloves garlic, minced

6 large basil leaves, chopped

3 tablespoons olive oil

½ teaspoon salt

1 (2 ¼ ounce) can olives, drained and sliced

1 cup Feta cheese, crumbled

Freshly ground pepper, to taste

1. The above measurements are good starters, but feel free to add more or less to taste. Cook pasta according to package directions. (If you're really feeling inspired, make your own pasta. All you need is Semolina flour, eggs, and olive oil.)

2. While the pasta is boiling, combine tomatoes, and next three ingredients. Salt the mixture and let the tomatoes soak up the salt for a few minutes. This will bring out the flavor of the tomatoes. (If heirloom tomatoes are in season, they will work great.)

3. Drain pasta and place in a large bowl. Top with tomato mixture, olives, and Feta cheese, then toss all together. Pepper to taste.

This recipe is a personal favorite because of how easy, fresh, and healthy it is!

K

Grilled Lime Chicken and Vegetables (recipe on p. 42)

Kebabs with
Cucumber Dipping Sauce
(recipe on p. 43)

41

GRILLED LIME CHICKEN AND VEGETABLES

GRILLED CHICKEN

PREP TIME: 15 minutes (plus at least 3 hours for refrigeration) | **COOK TIME:** 45 minutes | **SERVES:** 6

6 boneless, skinless chicken breasts

Juice from 1 lime

1 teaspoon lime zest

1 tablespoon honey

2 cloves garlic, minced

1 teaspoon fresh thyme, chopped

1 teaspoon salt

½ teaspoon pepper

2 tablespoons olive oil

Rosemary sprigs for decoration

1. Rinse the chicken breasts and pat dry.
2. In a medium bowl, mix lime juice, lime zest, honey, garlic, thyme, salt, pepper, and olive oil. Add the chicken breasts and coat well.
3. Cover and refrigerate chicken breasts for at least 3 hours (up to 6 hours).
4. Prepare the grill to medium-high heat. Grill the chicken breasts for about 5 minutes per side, along with the vegetables (see below).

GRILLED VEGETABLES

PREP TIME: 20 minutes | **COOK TIME:** 12 minutes | **SERVES:** 6

½ cup olive oil

1 clove garlic, crushed

Salt and pepper, to taste

2 zucchini

2 squash

8 new potatoes

1 bunch asparagus

1 eggplant

2 yellow bell peppers

Optional: Cherry tomatoes and/or 1 large tomato

Optional: Rosemary, to taste

Balsamic vinegar to drizzle

1. In a small bowl, mix the olive oil, garlic, salt, and pepper. Set aside.
2. **PREPARE VEGETABLES:** Cut zucchini and squash into 1/4-inch thick strips. Cut new potatoes in half. Cut the wooded ends off of the asparagus. Cut the eggplants into 1 1/2-inch thick slices. Cut bell peppers into quarters. If using cherry tomatoes, keep whole, and if using a larger tomato, cut in half.
3. Brush the vegetables with the oil mixture and transfer to a grill-safe vegetable basket.
4. Along with the chicken (see above), grill vegetables until brown, about 6 minutes per side.
5. Transfer to a platter and drizzle with balsamic vinegar.

KEBABS WITH CUCUMBER DIPPING SAUCE

CUCUMBER DIPPING SAUCE

PREP TIME: 10 minutes (plus 2 hours for refrigeration) | **COOK TIME:** 0 minutes | **SERVES:** 4–6

2 cups Greek yogurt

1 large cucumber, peeled, seeded, and chopped

salt and pepper, to taste

½ cup sour cream

2 tablespoons fresh lemon juice

2 tablespoons fresh dill, chopped

1 clove garlic, minced

1 tablespoon olive oil

1–2 packages pita bread

1. Mix all ingredients except the pita bread, and season with salt and pepper. Cover and chill in refrigerator for at least 2 hours.
2. Warm small pitas in the oven and serve with the dipping sauce.

LAMB KEBABS

PREP TIME: 15 minutes (plus 2 hours for refrigeration) | **COOK TIME:** 14–16 minutes | **SERVES:** 4–6

MARINADE

2 tablespoons olive oil

2 teaspoons lemon juice

2 cloves garlic, crushed

2 tablespoons parsley, chopped

LAMB

2 pounds lamb, top round, cut into cubes

1 large onion, cut into wedges

Sea salt, to taste

Freshly ground black pepper, to taste

1. Pulse all marinade ingredients in small food processor until smooth.
2. Pat the lamb dry and sprinkle generously with salt and pepper. Put lamb in a bowl, cover with the marinade, mix well. Then cover and refrigerate for up to 2 hours.
3. Preheat grill to medium-high heat. Take lamb out of refrigerator, and skewer the lamb chunks and onions in alternating fashion on metal skewers. Repeat until all ingredients are used. Oil the grill and place the kebabs on the grill. Grill for about 2 minutes per side, and repeat, alternating until meet is cooked (7–8 minutes total).

Pictured on page 41 ❖

BEEF KEBABS

PREP TIME: 15 minutes (plus 2 hours for refrigeration) | **COOK TIME:** 16 minutes | **SERVES:** 4–6

MARINADE

2 ½ tablespoons vegetable oil

2 tablespoons soy sauce

1 tablespoon lime juice

1 large clove garlic, finely
minced

¼ teaspoon black pepper

½ teaspoon salt

BEEF

1 pound sirloin, cut into cubes

1 ½ cup mushrooms, whole

1 large onion, peeled and cut
into wedges

1 red bell pepper, cut into
2-inch squares

1 green bell pepper, cut into
2-inch squares

1 yellow summer squash,
cut into ½-inch slices

1. Mix all marinade ingredients together in a medium bowl. Then add sirloin and toss well to coat. Cover and let sirloin marinate in the refrigerator for up to 2 hours. Once meat is finished marinating, add the vegetables to the bowl and mix well.

2. Skewer pieces of beef, mushroom, onion, green or red bell pepper, and yellow squash in alternating fashion on a metal skewer. Repeat until all the ingredients are used.

3. Preheat grill to medium-high heat and grill the kebabs for 2 minutes per side, alternating until meat is nicely browned (16 minutes total).

Summer Squash and Sausage Tomato Pasta (recipe on p. 48)

Stuffed Bell Peppers
(recipe on p. 49)

47

SUMMER SQUASH AND SAUSAGE TOMATO PASTA

PREP TIME: 15 minutes | **COOK TIME:** 30 minutes | **SERVES:** 6

2 medium to large squash

2 medium to large zucchini

2 pints, cherry tomatoes

4 tablespoons olive oil

Sea salt and freshly ground pepper, to taste

6 Italian sausage links

1 (16 ounce) package rigatoni pasta (substitute 1 box of quinoa for a gluten-free alternative)

Parmesan cheese for garnish

1. Chop squash and zucchini into bite-size squares and place in large bowl. Cut cherry tomatoes in half for a juicier sauce, or leave whole. Toss vegetables and tomatoes in 3 tablespoons olive oil, sea salt, and freshly ground pepper.

2. Swirl 1 tablespoon olive oil in a saucepan on high heat, and add sausage.

3. Once sausage is partially cooked, drain fat and then add the vegetables to the saucepan. Turn heat to medium. Cover the sausage and vegetables and allow to cook approximately 15 minutes.

4. While sausage and vegetables are cooking, boil water and cook pasta according to package directions.

5. When vegetables and sausage are cooked, remove sausage and cut each link into bite-size pieces, placing back into the saucepan once cut.

6. Once pasta is cooked, drain and place in large bowl. Serve pasta on individual plates and spoon sausage, vegetables, and tomatoes (and naturally occurring sauce) over pasta. Grate Parmesan cheese over each dish.

K *This is another one of my summer favorites when the vegetables are fresh. The sausage adds the perfect amount of flavor and richness to this recipe, and if you like a bit of spice, Italian sausage is a great option.*

❖ *Pictured on page 46*

STUFFED BELL PEPPERS

PREP TIME: 20 minutes | **COOK TIME:** 30–45 minutes | **SERVES:** 6

MEAT MIXTURE

3 teaspoons olive oil

1 medium onion, chopped

1 clove garlic, minced

1 pound ground beef

Salt and pepper, to taste

1 cup long grain rice, cooked according to package directions

6 bell peppers (choose a combination of colors)

Optional: ½ cup Mozzarella cheese

SAUCE

2 tablespoons butter

½ medium onion, chopped

1 clove garlic, minced

3 large Roma tomatoes, seeded and diced

1 (14 ounce) can tomato sauce

½ teaspoon basil, dried

½ tablespoon sugar

Salt and pepper, to taste

Optional: Hot pepper flakes

1. Heat the olive oil in a large skillet over medium heat. Add the onions and garlic, and cook for 3 minutes. Add the meat, salt, and pepper, breaking up the lumps until the meat is cooked through and just beginning to brown. Add the cooked rice. Cook in skillet until everything is heated through.

2. Cut off the tops of the bell peppers. Remove the seeds and discard the stems, but keep the tops intact. Fill peppers with meat-rice mixture and place top of pepper back on, securing with a toothpick.

3. **TO MAKE SAUCE:** Melt the butter in deep saucepan, at medium heat. Add the onion and garlic, and fry for 3 minutes, then add tomatoes and tomato sauce. Add basil, sugar, salt, and pepper. Add water if needed.

4. Once sauce is ready, add the stuffed peppers to the saucepan, standing up. Lower the heat and cook for about 30–45 minutes or until the peppers are soft. If you see that the sauce is drying, add a little bit of water.

ADAPTATION

For a kick, add a sprinkle of hot pepper flakes in the sauce! For a heartier version, add 1/2 cup of Mozzarella cheese in the meat-rice mixture.

I once took a trip down the Amazon where we visited a green bell pepper plantation. The people from the village kindly gave the cooks on our boat several bags of green bell peppers which showed up in every meal. So how could I not pass along Regina's version of this classic dish?

Pictured on page 47 ❖

Caprese Salad
(recipe on p. 52)

*Cucumber and Onion
with Sour Cream Salad
(recipe on p. 53)*

*BLT Towers
(recipe on p. 54)*

51

CAPRESE SALAD

PREP TIME: 15 minutes | **COOK TIME:** 0 | **SERVES:** 4–6

4 tomatoes (vine-ripened tomatoes or colorful heirloom tomatoes)

8 ounces fresh Mozzarella cheese (preferably packaged in water)

Sea salt and black pepper, to taste

8 basil leaves

Olive oil, to taste

Balsamic vinegar, to taste

1. Slice tomatoes and fresh Mozzarella.
2. Spread tomato slices on platter, and sprinkle with salt. On top of tomato slices, layer fresh Mozzarella and then add a layer of a basil leaf, repeating this pattern until all ingredients are used.
3. After layering, sprinkle with pepper; then drizzle with olive oil and balsamic vinegar. Serve room temperature, making sure to be creative with your presentation.
4. For a delightful presentation, add some greens to the plate or pile tomato slices and Mozzarella in the center of the plate, drizzled with olive oil and sea salt.

K *One of my favorite summer treats is sitting down to a fresh Caprese Salad with tomato and basil straight from my garden.*

❖ *Pictured on page 50*

CUCUMBER AND ONION WITH SOUR CREAM SALAD

PREP TIME: 1 hour and 20 minutes for refrigeration | **COOK TIME:** 0 minutes | **SERVES:** 4–6

2 medium cucumbers, sliced

½ large red onion, sliced thin

½ cup sour cream

2 tablespoons fresh dill, chopped

1 teaspoon chives, chopped

½ teaspoon white vinegar

Sugar, pinch

Salt and pepper, to taste

1. In a large bowl, mix the cucumbers and onions, and sprinkle with salt.
2. Cover with plastic wrap and refrigerate for about 1 hour.
3. Drain and discard the extra liquid from the cucumbers and onions. Place cucumbers and onions in a serving bowl.
4. In a small bowl, mix sour cream, fresh dill, chives, white vinegar, and sugar. Add the sour cream to the cucumber salad and toss to combine. Once combined, add salt and pepper, to taste.
5. Cover with plastic wrap and refrigerate for another 20 minutes.

If you don't like the strong taste of onion, you can make it milder by blanching the onion slices in boiling water for 1 minute, and then drop them in ice-cold water immediately after. It takes the sting out!

R

Pictured on page 51 ❖

BLT TOWERS

PREP TIME: 30 minutes | **COOK TIME:** 15 minutes | **SERVES:** 10–12

Bread slices, cut in rounds
(better if cut the same size
as the tomatoes)

3 tablespoons butter, melted

2 packages fresh Mozzarella
cheese, cut in ½-inch slices

10 small tomatoes, ends cut
off, sliced in ½-inch slices

1 large bunch bib lettuce,
cut in rounds

6 slices maple-glazed bacon,
fried crispy

1. Preheat oven to 350 degrees.
2. Using a circular cookie cutter, press into bread slices and create crustless bread rounds. Brush the rounds with butter, and toast in oven for about 8 minutes or until crispy.
3. Add Mozzarella to the bread round, then layer with tomato, lettuce, and bacon, making a tower. Repeat until all ingredients are used.
4. Secure the towers with a toothpick if desired, and place on platter. Easy and colorful!

These are mini BLTs in the cutest little bite-size presentations you've ever seen. They're colorful, tasty, and I bet they'll be the first appetizer to go at your gathering. Regina turned me onto these, and they're my new appetizer favorite.

BERRY TRIFLE

PREP TIME: 20 minutes | **COOK TIME:** 20 minutes | **SERVES:** 6–8

CUSTARD

1 can sweetened condensed
    milk

2 cans whole milk (use
    the empty sweetened
    condensed milk can for this)

4 egg yolks

¾ teaspoon vanilla

2 tablespoons corn starch

1 (8 ounce) can table cream

WHIPPING CREAM

2 cups whipping cream

BERRIES AND CAKE

4 tablespoons sugar

2 cups strawberries

2 cups blueberries

1 cup raspberries

1 cup blackberries

1 pound cake, cut into 1-inch
    squares (can be homemade
    or store-bought)

Berries and mint leaves
    for garnish

1. **TO MAKE CUSTARD:** In a medium saucepan, over medium heat, whisk together sweetened condensed milk, milk, egg yolks, vanilla, and corn starch. Whisk constantly and cook until the custard thickens into a pastry-cream consistency. Pour the custard into a bowl and add the table cream. Mix well and cover with plastic wrap, pressing it directly onto the surface of the cream to avoid forming a skin. Place in refrigerator to cool.

2. **TO MAKE WHIPPING CREAM:** Use an electric mixer to whip the whipping cream until stiff peaks form. Set aside.

3. **TO MAKE THE BERRIES:** Mix the sugar and all of the berries in a large bowl. To macerate and bring out the juices of the fruit, let the berry mixture stand for 30 minutes.

4. To assemble the trifle, add a layer of custard to the trifle bowl first. Then add a layer of cake, followed by a layer of the berry mixture and 3 tablespoons of fruit juice. Then add a layer of whipping cream. Repeat the prior step. Once the final layer of whipping cream is at the top of the trifle bowl, garnish with some berries and mint leaves. Set completed trifle in refrigerator for one hour.

ADAPTATIONS

You can also make a mini-trifle dessert using individual cups instead of a large trifle bowl. Also, ladyfingers (2 packages broken into 2-inch pieces) can be substituted for the pound cake.

GROWING HERBS

Nothing has made me appreciate cooking with fresh and seasonal ingredients like gardening. While planting and maintaining a prolific garden in your backyard may not be an option, growing a few herbs will go a long way in your cooking and entertaining. I'll start with some of my favorites: rosemary, sage, oregano, parsley, thyme, basil, cilantro, and mint. These are foundational herbs I plant in the spring, most of which will continue to grow into Thanksgiving. Some will even last through winter.

Perhaps the best thing about fresh herbs is that growing them is easy. So easy that the saying should be *easy as herbs* instead of *easy as pie*, because I've never found making pie to be as easy as growing herbs. Herbs tend to be hearty and aren't as temperamental as vegetables. I don't need to water them as often or look after them as closely as other plants. They tend to do their thing with little involvement, which is my kind of gardening. If you don't have the space in your yard for a large herb garden, you can plant some in a small raised bed or simply in pots with good gardening soil. Check each plant's label for watering and sunlight instructions, and start growing fresh herbs you can use year-round.

The most obvious reason for growing your own herbs is that they simply taste better than what you'll

There's another wonderful reason to grow your own herbs: it saves money.

typically find in the grocery store. I use fresh herbs to make stock and flavor soups, I sprinkle them over meats before roasting, and I toss them in sauces and slow cooker dishes. Fresh basil leaves are wonderful in Caprese Salads, bruschetta, and red sauces. And while cilantro doesn't like hot temperatures, I try to capitalize on its flavor in salsas, pico de gallo, and Mexican dishes during milder weather. Mint will positively take over your garden or pot, so be careful to trim back, but you can't beat the refreshing taste of fresh mint leaves in a cool drink, over yogurt with blueberries and honey, or mixed into a watermelon-with-Feta summer salad. Rosemary, with its hint of pine, is downright majestic in holiday dishes like roasted chicken, turkey, or lamb. Oregano, parsley, and thyme are magical in soup, given how savory they are. Because of its perfect balance of earthy and sweet, sage is fabulous with butternut squash ravioli, turkey dishes, and holiday dressings.

If you're still not convinced, there's another wonderful reason to grow your own herbs: it saves money. Have you noticed how expensive a plastic container of basil or cilantro is? Even dried herbs can add up. Whether you need a fresh stalk of a certain herb or a tablespoon of a dried one, growing herbs yourself is economical. (Drying herbs can be done several ways and is not difficult. Once you've harvested your herbs, do some research on drying them and choose the most conducive process.)

My favorite way to incorporate fresh herbs in my cooking is when I make dipping oil for bread. I combine freshly chopped herbs from my garden with high-quality olive oil onto a plate, and then grind sea salt and cracked pepper over top. If I'm really going for it, I add minced garlic. My favorite herbs for dipping oil are any combination of rosemary, oregano, thyme, sage, parsley, and basil. Serve this with warm, crusty bread, and you have a coveted option on your table that goes with just about anything.

So there you have it—all my favorite reasons for growing your own herbs. And I didn't even mention how impressed your guests will be that you cooked with the herbs you grew yourself. Just don't tell them how easy it is. ❖

THE
TOMATO

On my most recent trip to the Amazon, I asked my two favorite Brazilian cooks what their one go-to ingredient was.

Vilma quickly answered, *a cebola*, Portuguese for "the onion." Rosa was slightly more reflective, glancing away for a second but also coming back with, *a cebola*. I understand this. It's hard to do much of anything without an onion. Other ingredients like carrots, celery, and garlic could also give the onion a run for its money. They, too, help lay the foundation for so many recipes. And what would we do without staples like potatoes, rice, or beans? But let's really stop to think about this, folks—where in the world would we be as a species without the tomato? Chips and salsa? Gone. Pico de gallo? Out. Spaghetti? Forget it. Caprese Salad? Over. Fries and ketchup? Nope. Pizza? I can't even allow myself to travel the depths of such despair.

Where in the world would we be as a species without the tomato?

It was my dad who first instilled in me a love for the tomato. He had a fairly large garden in our backyard that was terribly unkempt. I can't believe he somehow slipped that heap of weeds and manure past my mom. He did manage an impressive yield of beef-steak tomatoes out of that eyesore, which may have been why he was able to get away with it. "Kelly, look at this beauty," he'd say, holding up a gargantuan specimen in both hands. "This thing has to be two pounds!" Then off he'd scurry to the kitchen to consume it over the sink using zero utensils. If my dad's tomatoes were part of our dinner, they'd be sliced up with salt and pepper. Nothing fancy. I don't remember adding basil or fresh mozzarella, even olive oil, to our tomatoes back then—at least not in our family. It's hard to imagine how I ever lived without the Caprese Salad.

My grandfather on my mom's side shared a similar love. Pulling through my Pop and Bammom's white stucco gates in south Florida, after an unbearable twenty-two hours on I-95 in our powder-blue station wagon with my three siblings, never lost its thrill. (Bammom is the unfortunate name I gave to my grandma because I couldn't pronounce *grandma*.) We'd wind up their driveway past the sprawling banyan tree and under the towering palm trees as the gravel crunched beneath our wheels. It was pure magic. Pop had grapefruit trees so prolific the branches sometimes snapped from the weight of their bounty. I was too young to appreciate his exploding lemon and lime trees—oh, the ways I would have put those orbs to work today. His palm trees were always heavy with coconuts and when the wind kicked up, they'd bomb the lawn. My Pop enjoyed every fruiting and flowering plant on his property, but if you wanted to find his heart, you'd have to follow him to his tomato garden.

Sometimes I'd sit next to him in the garden while his tomato plants drank from the hose in his hand. He was a relentless waterer, guiding it back and forth with the consistency of a swinging pendulum. Pop was never in a hurry— I have no idea how I descended from him. I seem to remember him preferring a fine nozzle at the end of his hose, one that threw an even mist across his shiny red beloveds.

The problem was that he had another beloved in his life—the woman he'd married.

"You know your Bammom keeps trying to get me to take a trip to Europe," he'd say. "But I'd rather stay here and watch my tomatoes grow."

I was too young to understand the chasm between taking a European excursion and watching your tomatoes grow. Today, I would have encouraged him to take that trip because the tomatoes would be there when he got back. Of course that wasn't really the point with my Pop. He was content with a daily routine and the simple joys of cultivating and meandering around his acreage.

While I don't remember either of my grandparents actually cooking with the tomatoes my Pop grew—they were a slice-them-up-and-salt-them kind of people like my dad—I have to believe my love for growing and cooking them has something to do with those early childhood memories at their home. It's a rare night that a tomato, in some form, doesn't show up in my dinner plan.

The tomato has continued to follow me, or more precisely I've followed it, all over the world. My mom took me to Italy during my freshman year of high school on my first mission trip. (If you're interested in missions, I highly recommend Italy, though you might ultimately end up in places like on a boat in the Amazon. So just go in knowing that God leads you where He wills.)

It was my first time out of the country and a trip my mom really wanted me to experience. I'm grateful to this day. Our dear friends Sam and Joan Fiore had moved from New Jersey and planted a church in Milan, and a group from our church was there to help get the word out. The Fiores' fledgling congregation was a couple years old and about thirty people in size. (It's now grown to a multicultural congregation of more than four hundred.) We passed out church invitations to passersby in the marketplace and sang songs in the piazzas. Sam shook his tambourine to get everyone's attention before he'd start preaching in the streets. Very few people can pull off a tambourine and a message to strangers about Jesus, but Sam was and still is one of them.

The church at Punto Lode was energetic and welcomed us with open Italian arms, feeding us with piles of pasta and, of course, every version of tomato sauce: Bolognese, a la vodka, pomodoro, arrabbiata.

The church at Punto Lode was energetic and welcomed us with open Italian arms, feeding us with piles of pasta and, of course, every version of tomato sauce: Bolognese, a la vodka, pomodoro, arrabbiata. We ate all of our meals in the small church hall, and though it's been more than twenty-five years, my vision of that room is as pristine as if I'd dropped by yesterday.

The strength of that memory is no doubt bolstered by the meals we ate there. Bread was served at every gathering and bowls of freshly grated Parmesan cheese and bottles of olive oil were always close at hand. It was the first time I'd ever eaten rigatoni with a la vodka sauce. To this day, I don't think I've ever had anything quite like it.

Part of the potency of that trip has to do with the way the ingredients taste in Italy. On a return visit many years later, I stood in Joan Fiore's kitchen while she made dinner for me and three of my closest friends.

"You know, my sauce doesn't taste as good in New Jersey as it does in Milan. It's something about the pork." She gave the boiling pasta another stir and looked back at me over her shoulder, "The problem is, you know, that the pigs in America aren't Italian pigs." She makes a valid point—what kind of flavor can we realistically expect out of a pig that doesn't speak Italian?

Everything just tastes better in Italy. While I contend that much of this has to do with the country's rich soil, as well as the recipes and cooking techniques passed down through the generations, so much of a meal's flavor is infused with the personalities and conversations around the table at which you're eating.

The stories of what Jesus is doing in Italy and in the people they minister to will keep you at the table past midnight.

Sam and Joan can make you laugh until you cry, but they can also just make you cry at the goodness of the Lord. The stories of what Jesus is doing in Italy and in the people they minister to will keep you at the table past midnight. For more than forty years they've served in a culture that was at one time very foreign to them, sacrificing the stability and comforts of home. I never leave a meal with Sam and Joan without feeling nourished in body and invigorated in spirit. If only I could regularly have such conversations about Jesus *with* the homemade tiramisu. But I think that's what heaven might be like.

Nashville is a far cry from Italy when it comes to Italian food, but we're doing the best we can. My brother David uses San Marzano tomatoes in his pizza sauce, a distinctly Italian approach for a good pizza. And it's so simple. We also have a good pizza dough recipe you'll love. Regina studied for a spell in Italy so she's bringing her specialties to the table as well. And, of course, throughout the cookbook, I'll be celebrating the tomato in all its various forms—cherry, Roma, vine-ripened, heirloom, you name it. Because the simple truth of the matter is that the tomato makes me happy. It's a symbol of summer in America, the hallmark of Italian food, and it reminds me of my dad and my Pop. And it just tastes good. *Buon appetito.* ❧

Rice Fritters
"Arancini"
(recipe on p. 70)

*Pansanella Salad
(recipe on p. 71)*

RICE FRITTERS "ARANCINI"

PREP TIME: 10 minutes | **COOK TIME:** 35 minutes | **SERVES:** 10

¼ cup butter

2 medium onions, finely chopped

2 cloves garlic, finely diced

3 cups Arborio rice

7 cups chicken stock, warm

1 cup Parmesan cheese, finely grated

2 medium eggs, beaten, for the rice mixture

½ cup bread crumbs

FILLING

1 ½ cups Fontina or Mozzarella cheese, cut into ½-inch cubes

BREADING

4 medium eggs, lightly beaten with a pinch of salt for the breading

4 ½ cups bread crumbs

3 cups vegetable oil, for frying

SALSA VERDE

3 tablespoons olive oil

1 teaspoon lemon zest

1 tablespoon capers, drained and chopped

⅓ cup parsley leaves, chopped

2 mint leaves, chopped

Salt and pepper, to taste

1. In a pan, melt the butter and sauté the onions and garlic over medium heat until soft, about 5 minutes.

2. Add the Arborio rice and stir until lightly toasted. Cook for 3 minutes and start, slowly, adding the chicken stock in 1/2 cup increments, stirring until each pour is absorbed by the rice and then adding more. Cook until the rice is al dente.

3. Remove the pan from the heat and add Parmesan cheese, 2 medium eggs, and 1/2 cup of bread crumbs. Let rest.

4. **TO FORM THE BALLS:** Spread a thin layer of the rice on the palm of your hand and place a cheese cube in the center. Close the rice around the cheese, patting it into a ball shape. Place the rice balls on a cookie sheet lined with parchment paper. Dip each ball in the beaten egg and roll in bread crumbs.

5. Heat the vegetable oil in a deep frying pan and dip the rice balls, a few at a time, cooking until lightly golden brown. Serve warm with a side of homemade marinara sauce or salsa verde.

6. **TO MAKE SALSA VERDE:** Add all ingredients together in a bowl. Mix well.

R
"Arancini" are small balls of rice that come from Sicily, where they are most commonly served as appetizers. They can be made with a variety of different fillings, including cheese, meat sauce, peas, sautéed mushrooms, prosciutto, or olives to name a few.

❖ *Pictured on page 68*

PANSANELLA SALAD

PREP TIME: 10 minutes (plus 30 minutes for refrigeration) | **COOK TIME:** 5–7 minutes | **SERVES:** 4–6

1 loaf of Italian crusty bread, cut into 1-inch cubes (2 ½ cups)

3 tablespoons olive oil

4 medium tomatoes, fresh, cut into 1-inch cubes

1 cucumber, unpeeled, seeded, and cut into cubes

½ cup red onion, diced

1 small red bell pepper, cut into cubes

10 fresh basil leaves, chopped

2 tablespoons capers, drained

Vinaigrette of your preference

1 teaspoon salt, more if needed

Black pepper, to taste

1. Preheat oven to 350 degrees. Toss the bread with olive oil, arrange on baking sheet, and bake for 5–7 minutes until toasted and crisp, making croutons. Set aside.

2. In a large bowl, mix the tomatoes, cucumbers, red onion, red bell pepper, basil leaves, and capers. Add the vinaigrette, salt, and pepper and toss together. Let the salad sit for at least 30 minutes to allow flavors to blend.

3. Add croutons before serving.

Pictured on page 69 ❖

SALMON WITH PESTO AND TOMATOES

PREP TIME: 15 minutes | **COOK TIME:** 20 minutes | **SERVES:** 6

3 cups fresh spinach, washed

4 tablespoons pesto, store-bought or homemade

6 skinless salmon fillets

1 pint cherry tomatoes, halved

2 cloves garlic, minced

1 teaspoon salt

1 teaspoon pepper

Balsamic vinegar, to taste

2 tablespoons olive oil

1 tablespoon fresh basil, chopped

Optional: You can substitute the spinach with zucchini, kale, or green beans.

1. Preheat oven to 375 degrees.
2. Lay the spinach in a casserole dish, and sprinkle with a bit of salt and pepper.
3. Spread the pesto on the pieces of salmon. Place them on top of the spinach.
4. In a bowl, mix the tomato halves with garlic, salt, pepper, and Balsamic vinegar, and place around the salmon.
5. Drizzle everything with olive oil and bake for about 20 minutes until the salmon is to your liking. Remove from oven and sprinkle with fresh basil.

I like this recipe because it's another way to serve salmon. The fresh pesto and tomatoes in the summer give salmon another showing. Pair with rice and a vegetable, and you have a well-rounded, healthy, easy meal.

Gnocchi with
Tomato Sauce
(recipe on p. 76)

Butternut Squash and
Sausage Risotto
(recipe on p. 77)

GNOCCHI WITH TOMATO SAUCE

PREP TIME: 50 minutes | **COOK TIME:** 45 minutes | **SERVES:** 4–6

GNOCCHI

3 large potatoes

1 egg

Salt, to taste

2 cups flour

TOMATO SAUCE

2 tablespoons olive oil

2 cloves garlic, minced

1 small onion, chopped

2 celery stalks, finely chopped

2 carrots, peeled and finely chopped

2 cans (32 ounces each) crushed tomato

Salt and pepper, to taste

3 basil leaves, chopped

½ teaspoon sugar

1. Cook the potatoes in water until tender. Drain, peel, and pass through the potato ricer. Place the potatoes in a large bowl and add the egg. Sprinkle with salt, and slowly add the flour, working with your hands, bringing the dough together. You want the dough to be smooth and elastic.

2. Divide the dough into 4 pieces or more. Shape each of the 4 pieces into a long roll, until each are 1/2 inch in diameter. Cut rolls into 1-inch pieces of gnocchi. Put pieces on a floured baking sheet and let sit.

3. Using a large pasta pot, boil water with 1 teaspoon of salt. Working in small batches, cook the gnocchi until they float to the top. Remove from water immediately with a slotted spoon to drain the water.

4. Serve with the tomato sauce below, or with browned butter and Parmesan cheese.

5. **TO MAKE TOMATO SAUCE:** Heat olive oil in a saucepan and add the garlic, onion, celery, and carrots, and sauté for a few minutes. Add the tomatoes, salt, pepper, basil, and sugar. Simmer for about 45 minutes until reduced a little and thickened. (You can leave the sauce chunky or you can puree.)

❖ *Pictured on page 74*

BUTTERNUT SQUASH AND SAUSAGE RISOTTO

PREP TIME: 20 minutes | **COOK TIME:** 30 minutes | **SERVES:** 6–8

1 large butternut squash, seeded and cubed (about 4 cups)

1 tablespoon olive oil

Salt and pepper, to taste

16 ounces ground sausage, casings removed

1 onion, diced

2 tablespoons butter

16 ounces Arborio rice

5 cups chicken stock

½ cup Parmesan cheese, grated

1. Preheat oven to 425 degrees. In a bowl, toss cubed butternut squash with olive oil, salt, and pepper. Place on baking sheet. Roast for 20–25 minutes until edges are lightly browned.

2. While squash cooks, brown the sausage in a pan, breaking up the meat with a wooden spoon. Drain most of the fat, keeping a small amount for flavor and set aside.

3. In a large saucepan, sauté onion with butter over medium heat for 3 minutes. Add rice and stir until well coated, about 2 minutes. Add 1 cup of stock and stir constantly until absorbed. Do this with each cup, waiting until stock is absorbed before adding the next cup. After 5 cups, if you feel like you can still add more liquid, add 1/2 cup of water (or stock) at a time until the rice is creamy and the texture is to your liking.

4. Once rice is cooked, add squash, sausage, and Parmesan cheese, stirring gently so squash stays intact.

5. Salt and pepper, to taste. Serve with a green vegetable such as asparagus or Brussels sprouts.

I ate this for the first time in Italy at my friend Nina's house. She whipped this up in less than 30 minutes and I've never forgotten it. I love serving this, especially in the fall and winter when you can use a warm and hearty dish.

K

Pictured on page 75 ❖

SPAGHETTI BOLOGNESE

PREP TIME: 20 minutes | **COOK TIME:** 55 minutes | **SERVES:** 4–6

3 tablespoons olive oil

2 cloves garlic, minced

1 large onion, chopped

2 medium carrots, peeled and chopped

½ pound ground beef

⅓ cup heavy cream

2 pounds tomatoes, peeled, seeded, and chopped

1 tablespoon tomato paste

Salt and pepper, to taste

1 ½ cups water

1 pound spaghetti

½ cup chives, chopped

½ cup parsley, chopped

Optional: Parmesan cheese

1. Heat the olive oil in a saucepan. Add minced garlic, onions, and carrots, and sauté until soft but not brown, stirring regularly. Add the ground beef and continue cooking, breaking up any lumps in meat with a wooden spoon. Sauté until meat is cooked.

2. Pour in the heavy cream and simmer gently until the liquid evaporates, about 6 minutes. Stir in the tomatoes, tomato paste, salt, pepper, and water. Simmer until the sauce is thick, stirring occasionally (about 40 minutes).

3. Cook the pasta in water with salt until al dente according to package directions. Drain the pasta and serve with the Bolognese sauce. Sprinkle with chives and parsley. Add Parmesan cheese if you desire.

There are few things more comforting than a slice of crusty bread and a bowl of Spaghetti Bolognese. The rich meat flavor sauce under a mountain of shaved Parmesan cheese takes me back to my childhood.

R

Tiramisu
(recipe on p. 82)

Berry Panna Cotta
(recipe on p. 83)

81

TIRAMISU

PREP TIME: 30 minutes | **COOK TIME:** 10 minutes | **SERVES:** 6–8

5 eggs, separated

¾ cup sugar

1 cup Mascarpone cheese

1 cup heavy cream

Salt, pinch

1 ½ cups brewed coffee

2 packages ladyfingers

Chocolate powder to decorate

1. **TO MAKE A SABAYON (TIRAMISU SAUCE):** Combine egg yolks and sugar in a double boiler with boiling water. On low heat, keep stirring and cooking for 10 minutes. Remove from heat and continue to whisk the yolk mixture until fluffy and light in color. Let rest for 5 minutes. Then, gently add the Mascarpone cheese to the yolk mixture and beat until well combined. Set aside.

2. **TO MAKE WHIPPING CREAM:** Use an electric mixer with whisk attachment to whisk the heavy cream until stiff peaks form. Then, add the whipping cream and salt to the tiramisu sauce, folding delicately. Set aside.

3. Create layer of ladyfingers on the bottom of a 9-inch square glass dish, or 9 x 10-inch rectangular glass dish. Using a pastry brush, brush a little of the coffee on each ladyfinger. Then add a layer of cream on top. Repeat this process 3 times. The top layer should be cream. Sprinkle with chocolate powder and refrigerate.

BERRY PANNA COTTA

PREP TIME: 15 minutes (plus 5 hours for refrigeration) | **COOK TIME:** 10 minutes | **SERVES:** 6

1 cup whole milk

1 package unflavored gelatin

3 cups whipping cream

¼ cup honey

1 ½ tablespoons sugar

Salt, pinch

3 cups strawberries, washed and cut into thirds

2 tablespoons sugar

1. Pour milk in a heavy saucepan. Sprinkle gelatin over top, and let stand for 6 minutes. Over medium heat, warm the saucepan until gelatin is dissolved (but do not allow the milk to boil), about 4–5 minutes.
2. Add the whipping cream, honey, sugar, and salt and stir until sugar dissolves.
3. Remove from heat and divide the cream into 6 dessert glasses. Cover with plastic wrap and refrigerate until set, about 5 hours.
4. In a medium bowl, mix the strawberries with 2 tablespoons of sugar and set aside.
5. When ready to serve, put 2 tablespoons of strawberries on top of each dessert.

Pictured on page 81 ❖

THE NEW
CHURCH
POTLUCK

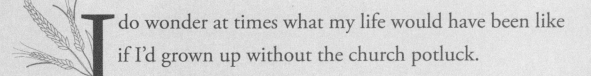

I do wonder at times what my life would have been like if I'd grown up without the church potluck.

It's hard to imagine a childhood without fellowship halls, fluorescent lighting, and foldout tables teeming with cheesy casseroles and buckets of fried chicken. Where the only green on anyone's plates was the Jell-O. (If you didn't grow up in church or a church culture like this one, have no fear, you probably consumed less cream of mushroom than I did.) It was an all-you-could-eat smorgasbord of carbohydrates and fried protein. I loved it so.

While I think that today we may place a greater emphasis on healthier eating habits—or at least we're more aware when we're eating something bad for us—I'm sentimental about the days where Bible study included eating something that contained gluten, corn syrup, or partially hydrogenated oil.

I have some really wonderful memories of gathering with the church body around meals for special occasions. Our annual Missions conferences were a highlight. Missionaries who were back on furlough had come from all over the world to tell us about what God was doing in the countries and cultures they were living in. Sometimes they'd give us a literal taste of the new place they called home, like the one missionary who flew in from the jungles of a part of the world I can't recall, and passed around a plate of charred worms. True story. The worms were apparently high in protein; I think this was against FDA regulations.

Whether it was the dessert receptions after special guests had spoken on a Sunday morning, or the ladies' Christmas brunch, or the week of pizza before the annual Easter cantata performances (that I grew up employing the word *cantata* in my regular vocabulary explains so much about my childhood), food was a significant part of my church experience. The habit of God's people gathering around food is as ancient as the stories in the Old and New Testaments. The annual Jewish festivals included both acts of worship and feasting together on the choicest cuts of meat. When we get to the Gospels, we read about Jesus eating with everyone from religious leaders to notorious sinners, with the healthy and with lepers. In Acts, we're given pictures of the early church praying and learning together in homes while breaking bread.

Many of these women were in the midst of walking through unspeakable trials and hardships. . . . The only reason they were able to love so well, and still show up to the fellowship hall with the lasagna, was because their roots ran deep in Christ.

The forms and foods have evolved over time, but the gathering and the eating have remained the same. We may have gone from fatted calves in the Old Testament, to shellfish with the dawning of the New Covenant, to chicken divan and boxed cake mixes in the 80s, to cheeseboards with chutney and prosciutto today, but it's God's people communing together that will always be most significant. While the church I grew up in had a few Legalistic Lisa's and Hypocritical Harry's, some of the best people I've ever known looked after me in those fellowship halls, around those tables, sometimes in the kitchens of their own homes: Linda Mitchell, Mary Wolfe, Michelle Smith, Suzie Linebaugh, Sherry Meddings, Cheryl Hurley, my mom. I'd put them up against anyone.

I didn't understand it at the time, but many of these women were in the midst of walking through unspeakable trials and hardships. (Some have greatly suffered since then, and are faithfully serving to this day.) The only reason they were able to love so well, and still show up to the fellowship hall with the lasagna, was because their roots ran deep in Christ. Looking back, while I was well-fed at their tables and at the church potlucks, it was their spiritual nourishment that would fortify me for decades to come.

Thinking back on those church gatherings and the meals we ate together, I don't feel as though my childhood suffered any real loss because we lacked things like marble charcuterie boards with Stilton cheese and fig preserves. I'm not sad that every table wasn't made of reclaimed

wood or that the fluorescent lighting wasn't a string of Edison bulbs instead. I don't really remember if we had flower arrangements in vintage vases. I absolutely love unique ingredients and beautiful serving pieces that make for inviting presentations, and I know many of the church moms I grew up with cared about these things too. It's just that I don't remember presentation basking under quite the same spotlight it does today.

In some ways, the social media age has galvanized our recipe options and hosting presentations, but in other ways it has held us to an impossible standard. (Admittedly, the bar was a little low during the Styrofoam plate and poppy seed chicken casserole days.) But who can nail a model home, reclaimed wood cheeseboard, fresh flower arrangement, marble appetizer slab, and farm-to-table menu every time we want to have a get-together? If we feel we have to produce magazine-worthy meals and place settings in order to have people over, we'll either join the materialism rat race where perfection is the only winner, or we'll shy away from opening up our homes entirely because we've prematurely disqualified ourselves.

Our food sophistication will be our deterrent if it robs us of our focus on people and what Jesus wants to do in our midst around the table.

When I consider what was important to my spiritual formation during my growing-up years in the church, it wasn't the Gruyère cheese puffs. Rather, it was the people who loved me with the patience and nurturing of Christ, often over meals. In the book of Deuteronomy, God told the people of Israel to teach their children about His ways when they woke up and went to bed and as they went about their days. I think this included while they gardened, cooked, and served the meals. I got this at the church potlucks and gatherings.

I adore a beautifully set table and a thoughtfully crafted meal. I appreciate, down to my bones, a clean kitchen and home. A quality cup of coffee with cream in a weighty diner mug will never be lost on me. If you brew it, I will come. But what has the power to change us, *really* change us, is Christ-centered community. There's no power in the presentation or even the food itself.

I used to get so caught up in serving local and organic dishes displayed on the most unique and beautiful pieces that sometimes I forgot about the most important ingredient—the people who would be coming. We may have swapped out Rice Krispy Treats for chocolate ganache and pizza bites for bruschetta, but our food sophistication will be our deterrent if it robs us of our focus on people and what Jesus wants to do in our midst around the table. After all, He's been known to show up over beans and rice.

I never want to lose sight of what God can accomplish through a meal around the table. On some days that's Will, Harper, and Lily at my kitchen island with pancakes and a juice box. On others, it's a fancy birthday celebration dinner, a last-minute get-together over pasta, or a group from church fellowshipping around the appetizers before Bible study.

If you come over I'll talk your ear off about whatever came from my garden or local farm, and I will point out every jam or tomato I canned. But what I hope you'll know when you leave is that you were loved in Jesus' name. And if you know that, it will stay with you ten thousand years past the day that marble cheeseboards and balsamic-glazed Brussels sprouts go out of style. ❧

I never want to lose sight of what God can accomplish through a meal around the table.

Charcuterie Board
(recipe on p. 94)

Asparagus with
Caper Tartlets
(recipe on p. 95)

CHARCUTERIE BOARD

PREP TIME: 45 minutes | **COOK TIME:** 0 minutes | **SERVES:** your preference

To make a beautiful charcuterie board, consider that you need a balanced mix of ingredients. Remember to mix up the textures. Fruits, nuts, and pickled ingredients are wonderful garnishes that complement the board. The board can be served as an appetizer or after a meal.

First, start with a large wooden, marble, or vintage board of your choice to set the ingredients on. Then add your choice of cheeses, meats, pâté, crackers and bread, pickled ingredients, fruit, and nuts from the lists seen below. The board can incorporate as many or as few ingredients as you choose, depending on your needs and preferences.

CHEESES (Choose 3 or 4 different varieties from the following)

French triple creamy cheese like Brie	Gruyère	Goat cheese
Firm Parmigiano Reggiano	Gouda	Aged Cheddar
	Gorgonzola	

MEATS (Choose 3 or 4 different varieties from the following)

Slices of prosciutto	Jamón serrano (Spanish ham)
Aged salami, sliced (sopressata, coppa, or any of your choice)	Mocetta (cured beef tenderloin)

PÂTÉ

Including pâté (French for *paste*, also called *terrine*) is a simple way to dress up a usual meat-and-cheese plate. You can put your choice of pâté in a beautiful petite bowl or form into shapes. Use your best pâté recipe, or just purchase in a local cheese store or your favorite specialty market.

CRACKERS AND BREAD

Choose your favorite type of crusty bread and crackers. Again, choose a variety for a pleasant presentation.

PICKLED OPTIONS

Pickled pearl onions	Olives
Pickled okra	Cornichons

❖ *Pictured on page 92*

FRUIT OPTIONS

Fresh figs	Pear slices
Campaign grapes	Apple slices

NUT OPTIONS

Whole Spanish almonds   Spiced pecans   Toasted walnuts

Charcuterie boards are so fun because you can be creative with them. No two need to be alike. You can pull items seasonally to craft whatever is flavorful and accessible.

K

ASPARAGUS WITH CAPER TARTLETS

PREP TIME: 20 minutes | **COOK TIME:** 5 minutes | **SERVES:** 12

1 pound asparagus

½ cup mayonnaise

1 tablespoon capers, chopped

1 ½ tablespoons lemon juice

½ clove garlic, crushed

4 hard boiled eggs, chopped

Salt and pepper, to taste

12 mini tartlets (store-bought or homemade)

FOR DECORATION

6 quail eggs, cooked

Asparagus tips

1 package sprouts, any type

1. Trim off woody ends of asparagus. Put asparagus on plate and cover with microwave-safe plastic wrap. Microwave 5 minutes, until cooked al dente.

2. Trim the tops off of the asparagus and reserve for decoration. Chop the remainder of asparagus very fine.

3. In a medium bowl, mix the chopped asparagus, mayonnaise, capers, lemon juice, garlic, eggs, salt, and pepper. Spoon the desired amount into each tartlet.

4. Decorate the top of the tartlet with tip of 1 asparagus, 1/2 cooked quail egg, and a couple of sprout sprigs on top.

        Pictured on page 93 ❖

SPRING ROLLS

PREP TIME: 45 minutes | **COOK TIME:** 0 minutes | **SERVES:** 6–8

PEANUT DIP

¾ cup peanut butter

2 tablespoons agave nectar

3 tablespoons coconut milk

Juice from 2 limes

½ cup soy sauce

2 teaspoons red chili paste

Decorative chopped peanuts,
  to top

SAUCE

1 clove garlic, minced

½ cup peanut butter

2 tablespoons sesame oil

4 tablespoons lime juice

½ teaspoon ginger, ground

2 tablespoons tamari sauce

1 tablespoon water, if needed

ROLLS

1 package rice paper

1 red bell pepper, julienned

1 yellow bell pepper, julienned

1 green bell pepper, julienned

1 zucchini, julienned

2 carrots, julienned

1 large cucumber, julienned

2 green onions, chopped

1 bib lettuce head, julienned

½ cup basil leaves, minced

Optional: 2 teaspoons roasted
  peanuts, chopped

1. **TO MAKE PEANUT DIP:** Combine all peanut dip ingredients except decorative chopped peanuts into a food processor or blender. Puree to combine. If more liquid is needed, add water or more coconut milk. Pour the sauce into a serving bowl and garnish with the chopped peanuts. Set aside.

2. **TO MAKE SAUCE:** Add all sauce ingredients to a food processor or blender and process until smooth. Add in water to create the sauce thickness you prefer. Set aside.

3. **TO MAKE SPRING ROLLS:** Prepare all ingredients for the roll, julienning the vegetables and chopping the peanuts. Toss all prepared ingredients together in a large bowl. Fill a large bowl with hot water. Lay a clean dish towel on top of a cutting board. Gently drop a rice paper wrapper into the water and keep it there for 10 seconds. Carefully transfer the wrapper to the dish towel.

4. Place mounds of the filling in the middle of the wrapper (be careful not to put too much filling that can tear the wrapper). Drizzle sauce on the filling, about 1 tablespoon per roll. Gently fold, first bringing the left and right sides toward the center. Then fold up the bottom side of the wrapper, and continue in that direction to roll it up. To keep it fresh while assembling the other spring rolls, put the first roll on a plate, and cover with a damp paper towel.

5. Serve immediately with peanut dip on the side.

Beef Crostini
(recipe on p. 100)

Shrimp Toast
with Aioli
(recipe on p. 100)

Corn Tartlets
(recipe on p. 101)

SHRIMP TOAST WITH AIOLI

PREP TIME: 20 minutes | **COOK TIME:** 15 minutes | **SERVES:** 12–14

SHRIMP AND TOAST

1 tablespoon butter

1 pound shrimp, raw, peeled, and deveined

Salt and pepper, to taste

1 clove garlic, crushed

½ tablespoon chives, chopped

½ tablespoon parsley, chopped

6–7 slices of white bread

AIOLI

½ cup mayonnaise

1 clove garlic, crushed

3 tablespoons lemon juice

½ teaspoon lemon zest

½ tablespoon chopped chives

Salt and pepper, to taste

1. Melt the butter in a saucepan; add the shrimp and the spices. Cook until shrimp is light pink.
2. Using a circular cookie cutter, press into slices of bread to create 2 circles per slice of bread. Brush each round with butter and then toast until golden.
3. **TO MAKE AIOLI:** Combine all aioli ingredients in a bowl.
4. Place 1 teaspoon aioli on each toast circle, then top each with a shrimp. Repeat until all ingredients are used. Serve cold.

BEEF CROSTINI

PREP TIME: 20 minutes | **COOK TIME:** 8–10 minutes | **SERVES:** 12–14

2 French baguettes, cut in slices on the diagonal

4 tablespoons olive oil

1 cup mayonnaise

½ teaspoon horseradish

Salt and pepper, to taste

1 beef tenderloin, roasted (or 2 pounds cooked roast beef)

1 bunch fresh arugula

1. Preheat the oven to 350 degrees.
2. Cover 1 or 2 baking sheets with parchment paper. On the sheet, arrange all the baguette slices side by side. Brush each slice with olive oil, let it toast until lightly golden (8–10 minutes), and then remove from oven.
3. In a small bowl, add mayonnaise, horseradish, salt, and pepper, and mix well.
4. Add a small scoop of mayonnaise and horseradish mixture onto a toasted baguette slice. Then top with 1 or 2 slices of beef, and garnish with a small arugula leaf.

CORN TARTLETS

PREP TIME: 20 minutes | **COOK TIME:** 0 minutes | **SERVES:** 10–12

2 cups frozen sweet corn,
thawed and drained

3 tablespoons mayonnaise

2 tablespoons sour cream

1 tablespoon chives, chopped

Salt and pepper, to taste

Store-bought cocktail cups,
wonton cups, small buttered
toasts, or pastry shells

1. In a large bowl, mix all the corn dip ingredients together.
2. Chill the mixture until ready to serve.
3. Place 1 teaspoon of the corn dip in each cup or shell, and place on a platter. Repeat until all ingredients are used.

These are a quick and easy appetizer for your sizzling summer parties. Serve the corn dip in pastry shells, wonton cups, or on lightly buttered toast. They tend to disappear quickly!

Pictured on page 99 ❖

FIESTA DIP

PREP TIME: 30 minutes | **COOK TIME:** 30 minutes | **SERVES:** 10–12

1 teaspoon olive oil

½ onion, chopped

1 clove garlic, minced

1 pound ground beef

Salt and pepper, to taste

1 package cream cheese, softened

1 (4 ounce) can green chilies

1 package mushrooms, diced

1 (15 ounce) can pinto beans

1 (14 ounce) jar salsa

2 cups Mozzarella cheese, grated

1 cup Cheddar cheese, grated

Bag of tortilla chips

1. Preheat oven to 350 degrees.
2. In a skillet, heat olive oil over medium-high heat. Add the onion and garlic and sauté for about 3 minutes.
3. Add the meat and cook, using a wooden spoon to break the meat apart. Add salt and pepper to taste and cook until done.
4. In a baking dish, layer the ingredients. Start with cream cheese, then ground beef, green chilies, mushrooms, pinto beans, salsa, Mozzarella, and Cheddar cheese.
5. Bake for about 30 minutes. Serve hot with tortilla chips.

REGINA'S BRAZILIAN PINTO BEANS

PREP TIME: 10 hours | **COOK TIME:** 1 hour | **SERVES:** 10–12

1 pound dry pinto beans

Water for soaking

3 tablespoons olive oil

1 cup bacon, cut into very small pieces

1 medium yellow onion, chopped

2 cloves of garlic, minced

1 tablespoon salt

8 cups water, or more if needed

1 bay leaf

Salt, to taste

½ teaspoon black pepper

1. First, soak the beans in a large bowl by bringing the water to 4 inches above the beans. Let stand overnight at room temperature.
2. In a Dutch oven over medium heat, fry the bacon in olive oil until crispy. Add onion and garlic, and let cook until onions are translucent. Drain the beans and add them to the Dutch oven, along with the 8 cups of water and the bay leaf. Cover, reduce heat to low, and let cook for 45 minutes, stirring occasionally. Add salt and pepper. Cook a little longer until the liquid thickens.
3. To finish, remove the bay leaf and serve over white rice.

Flatbreads Festival
(recipe on p. 106)

104

Shortbread Cookies
(recipe on p. 107)

FLATBREADS FESTIVAL

PREP TIME: 45 minutes (plus 1 hour for rising) | **COOK TIME:** 20 minutes | **SERVES:** 10–12

FLATBREAD

1 package yeast

½ teaspoon sugar

1 ¾ cup flour

1 teaspoon sea salt

¾ cup water, more if needed

1 teaspoon vegetable oil

Optional: Fresh thyme

Optional: Oregano, dried

INGREDIENT IDEAS FOR TOPPING

Beef: Aioli, slices of roast beef, Goat cheese pieces, arugula, a drizzle of olive oil.

Greek: Sliced avocados, shredded grilled chicken, cucumber slices, tomatoes, crumbled Feta cheese.

Peach: Ricotta, slices of fresh peach, peach jam, basil leaves, balsamic reduction drizzle.

Steak: Steak slices, grilled summer vegetables, olive oil, salt, and pepper.

Egg: Arugula, roasted red bell pepper strips, 2 eggs over easy, Pecorino Romano cheese.

Bacon and honey: Ricotta, crispy bacon drizzled with honey.

1. Add yeast, sugar, flour, salt, and thyme or oregano into a food processor. Pulse a couple of times to combine. Add water slowly until the dough begins to form a ball.

2. Take the dough out of the food processor. Knead by hand until the dough is smooth and elastic. Spray a bowl with vegetable oil and place the dough inside, cover with plastic wrap, and let rise for about 1 hour or until it doubles in size.

3. Punch the dough and then put on a floured surface. Cut into 10 equal pieces (or 20 pieces for minis).

4. With a rolling pin, roll out to form very flat circles or rectangles (1/2 inch thick).

5. Preheat indoor stovetop or outside grill to medium-high heat, and cook flatbread pieces until you see bubbles on the surface, about 1–2 minutes. Turn over and continue to cook 1–2 minutes more, or until bread has puffed up.

6. **TO ASSEMBLE FLATBREAD:** Layer toppings of choice on pieces of flatbread. Toast in oven if desired. Set on platter and serve warm or cold, depending on toppings.

Ⓡ
This is one of the simplest recipes for flatbread, but if you don't have the time to buy it at your grocery store. This makes 10 medium flatbreads or 20 minis.

❖ *Pictured on page 104*

SHORTBREAD COOKIES

PREP TIME: 20 minutes (plus 40 minutes for refrigeration) | **COOK TIME:** 16 minutes | **SERVES:** 12–18

SHORTBREAD

3 cups flour

⅝ cup sugar

½ cup butter

Vanilla extract, splash

1 egg yolk

FILLING OPTIONS

Guava paste

Chocolate ganache

Dulce de leche

Jam, personal preference

Granulated sugar for dusting

1. In a food processor, process all the shortbread ingredients until combined into dough.
2. Place the dough in a bowl, cover with plastic wrap, and refrigerate for about 30 minutes.
3. Preheat oven to 350 degrees.
4. On a lightly floured surface, roll the dough out to a 1/4-inch thickness. Cut rounds with a cookie cutter and place them on baking sheet lined with parchment paper. Refrigerate the cookies for about 10 minutes.
5. Bake for 16 minutes, or until you see the edges of the cookie start to turn lightly golden. Remove from the oven and set the cookies to cool on a wire rack.
6. Sandwich cookies with guava paste or other filling of your choice.
7. Roll each cookie in granulated sugar and serve or store in airtight container

This is my Brazilian recipe for shortbread that I've used for years! In my country, we use grams as measurements, but I've converted to cups for you to bring this sweet treat into your own home!

R

Pictured on page 105 ❖

FLOWERS, PLANTS, AND TABLE DÉCOR

If you come to my house for dinner you can expect that I've spent some time on the shopping and cooking, sometimes even sourcing my meat from local farmers. The problem is, I'm usually so immersed in the meal that I forget about ambience, table setting, and décor. Thankfully, I often have the help of my sister in-law, Megen, who is excellent at these things. I watch her kids; she gets my house ready. She may have the better deal. Here are a few tips I've picked up from her over the years.

Fresh flowers are the easiest and most beautiful way to create a rejuvenating ambience in your home. Without breaking the bank, you can start with filler greens like seeded eucalyptus, delphiniums, ferns, magnolia branches, Italian ruscus, and holly, all of which can fill out an arrangement so only a few flowers are needed to complete your décor. Combining filler greens—even the ones you clip from trees and plants in your yard—with seasonal flowers from your grocery store can go a long way on a budget.

While finding inexpensive flowers has become easier, even the cheaper options can add up after a while. That's why I decided to plant a cut flower garden this past year. Megen suggested zinnias, a flower particularly known for being unfussy, colorful, and prolific. She wasn't kidding. Hundreds grew in my backyard and the different varieties kept my indoor vases stocked and bright, all for the price of a pack of seeds. I also planted a pack of seeds that included several varieties so everything that came up was a bit of a surprise. I had fun clipping them and combining them into arrangements I set throughout my house. And the single, lone towering sunflower that peered down on the rest of my garden simply amused me, so I left it there to watch over the rest of the lot.

Hydrangeas are also relatively easy to grow, plus they're perennials so they come back year after year. Their puffy bursts of petals add texture and softness to any table. Of course there are knock-out roses, peonies, dianthus, tulips, begonias, and hundreds of others. Find what grows well in your area and see what works best for you. You'll love the joy and convenience of cutting a few stems and placing them in vases before a dinner party.

Megen suggested zinnias, a flower particularly known for being unfussy, colorful, and prolific. She wasn't kidding.

I also appreciate the way Megen repurposes family heirlooms in her home as containers for natural décor. She uses an old brass bowl to hold and display pinecones during the fall and greenery during the winter. She often creates large floral displays by placing various flower arrangements into small plastic cups, which are then tucked into beverage tubs. Or instead of using a large vase for flowers, she repurposes other items to hold them, one being an inexpensive blue and white bowl she found at an antique store. Combining meaningful pieces you already own with changing seasonal foliage is a simple way to keep your décor interesting without having to purchase new pieces on a regular basis.

For the tablescape, Megen selects a few tapered candleholders she loves and changes out the colors of the candles seasonally. She uses scraps from her favorite fabrics and turns them into simple table runners, again, alternating them seasonally. She likes to use woven chargers as an inexpensive option that brings texture to any table. Mixing metals is also a nice touch; for instance, incorporating brass napkin rings with your silverware. Last, if you have neutral dinner dishes that you love, you can always sprinkle in a little variety by adding small plates with different patterns.

When preparing your home for guests, the most important thing to remember is that you don't have to decorate elaborately or spend a lot of money. Use what nature offers you seasonally and bring it into your home. Try planting a pack of flower seeds and see what happens. Use your family and heirloom pieces to display your plants and greeneries. Light some candles for warmth and ambience. Be creative with texture, metals, and fabrics. And if all else fails, do what I do when Megen isn't available—just make a great meal and no one will remember what your house looked like. ❖

IN DEFENSE
OF SOUP

Let's talk about soup for a minute. For a while now I've been trying to analyze the reasons behind my soup obsession, to really understand it, since not everyone shares my enthusiasm.

For instance, when my brother, David; his wife, Megen; and their children moved to Nashville a few years ago, I wanted to help them get settled. Having them over for meals (especially on Sundays after church) was one way I could accomplish this. Naturally, I made soup. It was easy, I had plenty for everyone to have as much as they wanted, it made my house smell fabulous, and it simmered all day.

Never underestimate the presence of something simmering on your stovetop—it's the great by-product of soup making. The sound is like a bubbling brook running through your kitchen, only with an intoxicating smell and the promise of a nourishing and tasty meal. What is not to like about this?

My family really enjoyed my Kale, Sausage, and Cannellini Bean Soup the first time I served it. They liked the Chicken Noodle the second time. They were sort of okay with the Turkey Vegetable after Thanksgiving. By the time soup dinners four and five rolled around, they were bringing their own tacos from the Mexican restaurant up the street. There was even an occasion when my brother and I were talking on the phone about the following night's dinner plan when he asked, "Megen wants to know if you're making soup." This was code for *we're probably not coming if you are.* I was being placed on soup detention by my own family members!

I was being placed on soup detention by my own family members!

Come to find out, my family members weren't the only ones behind this kitchen coup. My friends were boycotting my soups as well. It's not that they didn't enjoy my soup; it's just that for a time, it was the only thing I was making. My five-year-old niece Harper was the one woman I had in my corner. She adores my chicken soup. (Will doesn't like it, but only because he says he's allergic to chicken and I can't be held responsible for this.) Harper does have one bone to pick with my chicken soup though, and incidentally, it's the bones.

Because I always make my own chicken broth, it's not unusual to find an accidental bone or two in the soup. Harper has a knack for discovering them. "Kelly, how come there's always *bones* in your soup?" she sighs.

My response is always, "Because chickens have bones!" The other reason, of course, is that sometimes I'm rushing and don't get all of them out. But the reason behind that reason is that *chickens actually have bones* and you wouldn't believe how many little kids don't know this. I'm training them at my table. As long as what's in their bowls taste good, they don't seem to mind.

I will give some credit to my mom for my love of soup. She's always made great broths and continues to serve it to my nieces and nephews in Virginia who can flat put *down* some bowls of her Pasta Fagioli or 12 Bean Soup. She always feels good about this because not only do they enjoy it, but they're also being nourished with healthy ingredients.

Besides all the comforting properties of soup, the health benefits of homemade chicken or beef broth are astounding and numerous. The gelatin from the bones has been said to help with digestion, skin diseases, flus, colds, and joint problems. Dr. Pottenger, who pioneered the use of gelatin-rich broths, wrote an article in 1938 where he claimed, "the most important piece of equipment in any kitchen is the stockpot."* See, I even had support from the nineteen-thirties.

I went back even further and did a search for soup in the Bible. I found that soup is only mentioned in the Old Testament, and unfortunately not under the cheeriest of circumstances. Esau bitterly traded his birthright for a bowl of soup that his brother Jacob had made. The ensuing decades of tumult and acrimony between these two brothers can all be traced back to the soup. I found this all very discouraging, so I kept researching.

I came across Elisha who served soup to his men during a famine, and when they ate it they cried, "there's death in the pot." So that was just awful. I then found that soup is also mentioned in Ezekiel as a metaphor for God's judgment upon Israel. Tip: never invite someone over for Judgment Soup. To recap: soup was the only meal in the Old Testament to show up in stories of betrayal, famine, and judgment. This wasn't helping my cause.

Although I couldn't find the direct support that's often given to bread, fish, figs, or honey, I found lots of indirect support that I want to share with you. For one thing, soup is a relaxed and accessible dish as we seek to invite people into our homes. No one needs to dress up for soup. Soup says, "Come as you are." Soup is nothing if not disarming.

No one needs to dress up for soup. Soup says, "Come as you are." Soup is nothing if not disarming.

As I've been thinking about cooking and eating together especially in the context of the Christian faith, I've become more aware of how many transformative discussions took place around a meal with Jesus, and how we need to make room for more of these. The meals we share together have the power to encourage, challenge, bless, and heal, if governed by the Holy Spirit. How many times have you walked away from someone's house after sharing a cup of coffee or a hearty dinner and thought, *I really needed that*? You probably weren't thinking of the caffeine or the eggplant parmesan, rather the communion you shared with that person. In an unprecedentedly busy society, we need meaningful interactions and conversations with one another more than ever. While making soup may not be quite as convenient as the drive-through window, it's one of the easier options that still allows you to have people in your home for something homemade.

In other words, when I want to have people over for meaningful engagement, but don't have the time to try my hand at the Brazilian Feijoada, I can make soup. And people will still come. (Unless you're my family.) If it's a Mexican or bean soup, you can pair it with chips and salsa, maybe some guacamole. If it's something like beef farro, a warm loaf of crusty bread with dipping oil and herbs is always a hit. And you can never go wrong by pairing Tomato Basil Soup with a simple grilled cheese sandwich. Soup is a way to put a meal together that's not terribly involved, fosters community, and brings people into your home.

In our environmentally conscious world, I also find soup to be economical and a thorough use of our resources. Whenever I'm in Brazil and the indigenous cooks from the jungle prepare meals for us, nothing goes to waste because bones and excess ingredients can always be turned into soup. What may have been thrown away in our kitchen is the stuff of gold for a hearty soup in other parts of the world. While I'm in Brazil, if roasted chicken and vegetables are

served on a Monday, I know the soup of my life is coming on Tuesday. Tossing a chicken carcass and leftover vegetables into a stockpot is not only responsible and wonderfully resourceful; it's healthy and just plain flavorful.

I've found the stockpot to be the most welcoming, indiscriminate option for any leftover ingredients you can't otherwise find a place for. The other night I made salsa verde chicken enchiladas and used bone-in thighs. Instead of throwing out the bones and the bits of chicken stuck to the bones, I threw them in a pot and let them simmer for a few hours with leftover onion and herb stalks. By the end of the night I had both chicken enchiladas and a big bowl of broth I was able to use when making a side dish of rice and also for subsequent meals. Soup is just good economy, not to mention as comforting as a grandmother knitting in a rocking chair or a pair of warm socks.

So there you have it. My defense for all the soup. It makes every crevice of your home smell inviting. It's a way to offer your table like Jesus offers His to us. It's healthy, economical, tastes good, can be eaten as leftovers for several days, feeds a lot of people, and simmers on the stove while you go about your day. Soup is an ever-present reminder that there are still some things that are right with the world. ✄

It's a way to offer your table like Jesus offers His to us.

---

* Sally Fallon Morell and Kaayla T. Daniel, *Nourishing Broth: An Old-Fashioned Remedy for the Modern World* (Grand Central Publishing, September 30, 2014).

KALE, SAUSAGE, AND CANNELLINI BEAN SOUP

PREP TIME: 20 minutes | **COOK TIME:** 50 minutes | **SERVES:** 4–6

¼ cup extra virgin olive oil

6–8 cloves garlic, minced

2 teaspoons oregano, dried

2 tablespoons red wine vinegar

1 (6 ounce) can tomato paste

2 (15 ounces each) cans cannellini beans, drained and rinsed

2 ½ quarts chicken stock (add more for brothier soup)

Salt and pepper, to taste

1 pound Italian sausage links (or ground sausage)

1 bunch kale, large ribs removed and chopped

Parmesan cheese, shaved to taste for garnish

1. Heat the extra virgin olive oil in a large pot over medium heat. Add garlic and oregano and cook until garlic is translucent, around 3 minutes. Be careful not to burn.

2. Add vinegar and tomato paste. Cook another minute until the oil and paste has blended together.

3. Add rinsed beans and stock and bring to a simmer for 30–45 minutes. Season with salt and pepper, to taste.

4. While the soup is simmering, in another pan, partially cook the sausage links (you can also use ground sausage). Once halfway cooked, let sausage cool. Then slice into bite-size pieces and toss them into the soup where they finish cooking. (Allowing the sausage to finish cooking in the soup creates a fuller flavor in the broth.)

5. Add kale and simmer, partially covered, for another 15–30 minutes, making sure the sausage is thoroughly cooked.

6. Garnish with fresh shaved Parmesan cheese.

I like to eat healthy broths and vegetables, but occasionally you can't beat sausage. This is a great recipe that gives you your beans and kale, but doesn't skimp on tasting great.

K

Tomato Basil Soup
(recipe on p. 122)

3-Cheese Grilled
Cheese Sandwich
(recipe on p. 124)

Beef Farro Soup
(recipe on p. 123)

TOMATO BASIL SOUP

PREP TIME: 15 minutes | **COOK TIME:** 1 hour 15 minutes | **SERVES:** 5–7

14 ripe tomatoes, cut in half, stems removed

2 tablespoons olive oil

1 clove garlic, quartered

2 ½ cups chicken stock

1 tablespoon sugar

Salt and pepper, to taste

Optional: 1 cup heavy cream (if creamy soup is desired)

Basil leaves, handful

1. Preheat oven to 350 degrees.
2. On a baking sheet, place the tomatoes in one layer, drizzle with olive oil, and bake for about 30–40 minutes until soft.
3. Place the tomatoes, garlic, chicken stock, and sugar in a food processor and process until smooth, making the soup.
4. Put the soup in a saucepan and let it cook for 30 minutes on medium-low heat.
5. Salt and pepper to taste. If a creamy soup is desired, add heavy cream. Pour into bowls for serving.
6. Decorate each bowl of soup with a basil leaf. Serve alongside a yummy grilled cheese sandwich (see p. 124).

There are two secrets to a delicious tomato soup. First is the freshness and the ripeness of the tomatoes (try to get them in season at your farmer's market). Second is to bake the tomatoes instead of sautéing them.

❖ *Pictured on page 120*

BEEF FARRO SOUP

PREP TIME: 15 minutes | **COOK TIME:** 2–4 hours | **SERVES:** 6–8

3 tablespoons flour

2 teaspoons salt

½ teaspoon pepper

2 pounds boneless beef roast, cut into 1-inch cubes

2 tablespoons vegetable oil

3 cups yellow onions, sliced

2 medium cloves garlic, crushed

1 teaspoon Worcestershire sauce

½ teaspoon dried thyme

2 Russet potatoes, peeled and cut into 1 ½-inch pieces

3 medium carrots, peeled and cut diagonally into 1-inch pieces

1 cup farro

1 (10 ounce) bag frozen peas

1 (10 ounce) bag frozen corn

2 tablespoons fresh parsley, chopped

1. Combine flour, salt, and pepper in a bowl and dredge beef in flour mixture.
2. Heat 1/2 of the vegetable oil in Dutch oven over medium heat. Add half of the beef, cook until browned all over, about 5–6 minutes. Transfer to a bowl. Repeat with the remaining vegetable oil and beef.
3. Add onion and garlic and cook in Dutch oven until softened.
4. Add beef, Worcestershire sauce, and thyme and cover. Bring to a boil and reduce heat to medium-low. Simmer until beef is tender (2–3 hours).
5. Stir in potatoes, carrots, and farro and cook for another 30 minutes until carrots are tender. Add peas and corn, and cook an additional 5 minutes.
6. Pour soup into bowls and top each serving with chopped parsley.

Pictured on page 121 ❖

3-CHEESE GRILLED CHEESE SANDWICH

PREP TIME: 10 minutes | **COOK TIME:** 8 minutes | **SERVES:** 4

8 slices Italian or French crusty bread

3 tablespoons butter

4 slices Mozzarella cheese

4 slices Asiago cheese

4 slices Monterey Jack cheese

1. Preheat skillet over medium heat and generously butter one side of the bread.

2. Place bread butter-side down onto skillet and add the 3 slices of cheese. Butter the other slice of bread and place butter-side up on top of the cheese.

3. Grill until lightly brown and flip over. Continue grilling until cheese is melted (approximately 4 minutes per side). Repeat with the other sandwiches. Serve along with Tomato Basil soup (see p. 122), or any soup of your choice.

❖ *Pictured on page 120*

CORNBREAD

PREP TIME: 20 minutes | **COOK TIME:** 35–40 minutes | **SERVES:** 4–6

¾ cup vegetable oil

3 eggs

1 cup canned creamed corn

1 ½ cups sour cream

1 ½ cups cornbread mix

Salt, pinch

1 teaspoon baking powder

1 tablespoon jalapeño, chopped

2 tablespoons sugar

1. Preheat oven to 350 degrees.
2. Mix vegetable oil, eggs, creamed corn, sour cream, cornbread mix, salt, baking powder, jalapeño, and sugar in a bowl.
3. Spray a 9 x 12-inch baking dish with cooking spray. Pour the batter into the pan and bake for 35–40 minutes. Serve along with Chili (see p. 128), or any soup of your choice.

I got the cornbread recipe from a friend a long time ago. The sour cream makes it so moist!

Ⓚ

Pictured on page 126 ❖

Cornbread
(recipe on p. 125)

Chili
(recipe on p. 128)

Salsa Verde
Chicken Soup
(recipe on p. 129)

CHILI

PREP TIME: 20 minutes | **COOK TIME:** 4 hours | **SERVES:** 4–6

2 tablespoons olive oil

1 ½ pounds ground beef

16 ounces chuck roast,
  cut in small cubes

1 large onion, chopped

1 large clove garlic, minced

½ cup celery, chopped

1 (16 ounce) can kidney beans

1 (16 ounce) can pinto beans or
  black beans

1 (14 ounce) can diced
  tomatoes

4 tablespoons tomato paste

Salt and pepper, to taste

2 tablespoons chili powder

1 tablespoon dried mustard

2 cups beef broth

Sour cream

Shredded cheese (any kind you
  choose)

1. Place 1 tablespoon olive oil and the ground beef in a skillet over medium-high heat and cook, stirring constantly, breaking up the meat. Empty skillet and set beef aside.

2. In the same skillet, add another tablespoon of olive oil and fry the chuck roast pieces until brown on all sides.

3. In a large Crock-Pot (or soup pot), add all the ingredients with the meats. Cook for at least 4 hours on medium-low. Check for flavor, adding more salt or chili powder if needed.

4. Serve with sour cream and shredded cheese of your choice.

❖ *Pictured on page 126*

SALSA VERDE CHICKEN SOUP

PREP TIME: 15 minutes | **COOK TIME:** 20 minutes | **SERVES:** 6–8

1 (12 ounce) can salsa verde

3 cups rotisserie chicken

1 (15 ounce) can cannellini
beans, drained

3 cups chicken broth (or more if
soupier texture is desired)

1 teaspoon cumin, ground

½ package (10 ounce) frozen
corn

1 teaspoon chili powder

2 green onions, chopped

Sour cream

Bag of tortilla chips

1. Empty salsa verde into a large soup pot. Cook 2 minutes over medium-high heat.
2. Then add chicken, beans, broth, cumin, corn, and chili powder to saucepan. Bring to a boil, lower the heat to simmer and cook 10 minutes, stirring occasionally.
3. Top each bowl with onions, sour cream, and chips.

My friend Mary Katharine makes this at least twice a football season. It's like drinking your salsa except better. Topped with sour cream and tortilla chips, even if you don't like football, you'll love this soup.

K

Pictured on page 127 ❖

BUTTERNUT BISQUE WITH APPLE CROUTONS

PREP TIME: 20 minutes | **COOK TIME:** 40 minutes | **SERVES:** 6–8

SOUP

3 slices bacon, cooked and crumbled (reserve the fat)

1 cup onion, chopped

1 clove garlic, minced

6 cups butternut squash, peeled and cubed

2 apples, peeled and cubed

4 cups chicken broth

Salt and pepper, to taste

½ cup heavy cream

CROUTONS

10 slices French bread

¼ cup apple butter

3 tablespoons sugar

¾ teaspoon cinnamon

1. In a soup pot, add the bacon fat and onion. Sauté for 2 minutes, then add garlic, squash, apples, and chicken broth. Salt and pepper, to taste. Simmer, covered, until squash is very tender.

2. Remove from heat and puree soup in blender (or use immersion blender). Then transfer back to the soup pot, and add more chicken broth if needed. Just before serving, stir in the bacon and heavy cream.

3. **TO MAKE CROUTONS:** Preheat oven to 350 degrees.

4. Cut the bread into crouton shape. Toss croutons with the apple butter and sprinkle with sugar and cinnamon. Place on a baking sheet and bake for 10 minutes.

5. Shake the baking sheet, turning the croutons around, and bake for another 10 minutes.

6. Remove from oven and add croutons to soup bowls.

Turkey Rice Soup
(recipe on p. 134)

*Two-Day Chicken
Noodle Soup
(recipe on p. 135)*

133

TURKEY RICE SOUP

PREP TIME: 15 minutes | **COOK TIME:** 2 hours 35 minutes | **SERVES:** 4–6

Turkey carcass

2 stalks celery, chopped

2 carrots, peeled and sliced

1 onion, diced

1 clove garlic, minced

2 quarts chicken broth

Salt and pepper, to taste

2 cups rice

1 (10 ounce) package frozen peas

1 (10 ounce) package frozen corn

1. Combine the turkey carcass, celery, carrots, onion, garlic, chicken broth, salt, and pepper in a soup pot and let it simmer for 2 hours. Add more broth or water if needed. (Skim off the foam that sometimes forms on top of the pot.)

2. Pass the soup through a strainer, ensuring that you capture the broth, and return the broth to the pot.

3. Examine the carcass for any pieces of meat, tear off, and return them to pot. Once all meat has been torn off, discard all bones and skin.

4. Add the rice and cook for 15–20 minutes. Then add the peas and corn, and simmer for 15 more minutes, ensuring that the rice is cooked.

If you ever come to my house the day after Thanksgiving I can guarantee you a bowl of this soup. I love boiling the turkey carcass for stock and then adding leftover pieces of turkey, vegetables, and rice for one of the most comforting and nourishing soups I enjoy all year.

❖ *Pictured on page 132*

TWO-DAY CHICKEN NOODLE SOUP

PREP TIME: 20 minutes | **COOK TIME:** 1 hour 50 minutes | **SERVES:** 4–6

1 whole chicken, raw

1 cup celery, chopped

1 onion, chopped

6 carrots, chopped

½ pound egg noodles

Salt and pepper, to taste

¼ cup parsley, chopped

DAY 1

1. Wash the chicken, place in a large pot, cover with water, and boil 50 minutes. Remove chicken and strain the broth.
2. Remove cooked chicken from bone, cut into pieces or shred, and store in refrigerator overnight.
3. Return bones to liquid in pot and gently boil for 1 hour.
4. Separate the liquid from the solids by pouring through a sieve. Discard bones.
5. Cover broth and refrigerate overnight (store in separate container from the chicken).

DAY 2

1. Overnight, a layer of fat will have risen to the top of the broth. Remove and discard the fat.
2. Cook chopped celery, onion, and carrots in a small amount of water over medium-high heat until soft. Add broth to vegetables and heat through.
3. Meanwhile, cook the noodles separately according to the package directions until al dente. Drain and add to the broth.
4. Taste soup and season with salt and pepper, and half of the parsley. Stir in reserved chicken. Taste again for seasoning.
5. Heat until warmed through. Sprinkle the remaining parsley to serve.

Pictured on page 133 ❖

HOMEMADE STOCK

I love making my own stock for soups, sauces, and gravies. A good stock in your soup is like the highest quality cream in your butter, the finest cocoa in your chocolate torte, the ripest San Marzanos in your pizza sauce. Sure, you can buy stock in a box or can from the grocery store, but in Regina's words, "Believe me, there is nothing like a good homemade beef or chicken stock, like the ones my grandmother and mother used to make." Stock is the soul of your soup, so you don't want to skimp here.

> ## Stock is the soul of your soup, so you don't want to skimp here.

The health benefits of bone broth are immeasurable. The collagen, gelatin, and amino acids from the bones help fight inflammation, joint pain, and alleviate colds. In addition, the texture of homemade broth is nuanced and the flavor is nothing if not comforting. Perhaps most important, making your own stock makes you feel over-achieverish. And sometimes it's nice to feel this way.

To make my own chicken broth, I bring a whole chicken to room temperature, place it in a stockpot, and cover with water. Once I bring the water to a boil, I turn it down to a simmer and cover the pot for about an hour. I periodically check the pot and skim the foam off the top. Once the chicken is cooked, I remove it from the stockpot and set aside on a large plate or cutting board. After the chicken has cooled I remove the meat and tear it into bite-size pieces. I then refrigerate the meat.

Next, I return all the bones and carcass back to the stockpot, adding 3–5 roughly cut carrots, a couple celery stalks, a quartered onion, and any handful of herb stalks from my garden. I let the bones and vegetables simmer another few hours. (Optional: adding a little apple cider vinegar to your stock helps pull the nutrients out of the bones.) I may add salt and pepper at this point, too, but you can wait until later.

After a few hours, I remove all the bones and vegetables from the pot. If I'm making chicken soup that day I return the refrigerated chicken meat to the pot, add some seasoning, and I'm ready to serve a meal everyone is excited about. Otherwise, I can use the chicken in a separate meal for that day, and then freeze or refrigerate the fresh stock for another day.

If you're looking for a beef stock, here's Regina's recipe I recommend trying on a cold winter's day. ❖

REGINA'S BEEF STOCK

PREP TIME: 1 hour | **COOK TIME:** 2–3 hours | **SERVING SIZE:** 2–3 quarts

BOUQUET GARNI

2 fresh rosemary sprigs

4 fresh thyme sprigs

2 dried bay leaves

1 tablespoon black
  peppercorns, whole

BEEF STOCK

1 ½ beef bones (ask your
  butcher to cut the bones
  into small pieces)

1 pound beef stew meat

2 large onions, cubed

3 large carrots, cut into thirds

2 celery stalks, cut into thirds

6 quarts water

1. Preheat the oven to 450 degrees.

2. **MAKE A BOUQUET GARNI:** Put the rosemary, thyme, bay leaves, and peppercorns on a cheese cloth. Wrap the cheese cloth around these ingredients, and secure it so that the bouquet can float around the stock to flavor it.

3. Place the bones, beef stew meat, onions, carrots, and celery on a roasting pan. Roast in the oven, turning occasionally, until the vegetables and bones are deep brown, about 1 hour. Transfer to a large stockpot and reserve.

4. Place the roasting pan on the stovetop and bring to high heat. Stir to remove the browned bits from the bottom of the pan. Pour the bits into the stockpot.

5. Add 6 quarts of water to cover the bones. Cover and bring to a boil. Skim any foam as it comes to the surface. Reduce the heat to a gentle simmer and add the bouquet garni to flavor the broth. Simmer for about 2–3 hours, skimming off the foam again, if needed.

6. After several hours of simmering, strain the stock thorough a fine sieve; then discard the solids and the bouquet garni. Let the stock cool and transfer to an airtight container and refrigerate.

I know what you're thinking: What in the world is a bouquet garni? Because that's what I'm thinking. A bouquet garni is a French term, and it's a bundle of herbs typically used for making broths. Just so we're clear: it is pulled out of the stock before consumption.

A BIG FISH
STORY FROM
THE AMAZON

Nearly ten years ago I took my first trip to the Amazon jungle with Justice & Mercy International. Even after twenty trips (and counting), I've never gotten over the *ribeirinhos* (Portuguese for "river people"), their culture, or their food.

Oddly enough, it was precisely the food part I was most nervous about when preparing for my inaugural venture down the Amazon. When living on a riverboat for a week, one strung with hammocks and called *The Discovery*, what kinds of meals is one served? And how much discovering did I want to be doing in the way of food? This all felt a little suspect to me. So I did what any normal American would do. I packed enough energy bars and crunchy peanut butter to sustain me into my seventies.

Brazilians really detest peanut butter, by the way. Beyond all the cultural differences I've noted between our respective countries, I find the peanut butter divide the most troubling. The upside, though, is that no one there ever asks if they can have some of yours. But who knew that not even *I* would need to crack open my lid of legumes that first week in the Amazon? Not when there were endless varieties of bananas, passion fruit, coconuts, mangoes, and pineapples abounding at every turn. Not when we were floating down the world's largest river teeming with tambaqui, piraricu, and piranha. Even beans and rice had gone from normal fare to Brazilian flare.

I became an early adapter of *farofa*, a crunchy substance that comes from the manioc root, a staple Brazilians work into just about everything. It's hard to find here in America, so I go to

Regina's when I'm missing the Amazon—she always has a stash on hand. Our cooks on the boat, Rosa and Vilma, dazzled us with their nightly desserts of mousses, flans, and cakes made with their traditional fruits. I quickly became a regular Brazilian food enthusiast. (It's important to note that I did have to draw the line somewhere. I find their pizza to be a betrayal of all things good and beautiful—they top it with mayonnaise, hardboiled eggs, raw onion, deli meats, and olives. So, there's this small issue of them having ruined pizza, but besides that . . .)

The tricky thing about the food in the Amazon region (distinct from the city of Manaus) is that most of the people, as I've previously mentioned, live solely off the land and river where the resources vary seasonally. The Amazon River floods the land during the rainy season and it's an annual occurrence, swelling anywhere from seven to fifteen meters. Those who live in these flood basins routinely look forward to their crops being destroyed and the fish becoming troublingly scarce. The question is not if it will happen, but how bad it will be. No matter how many times I visit the Amazon, I never get over the plight of those who must face their food sources being wiped out on a yearly and expected basis.

Much of the work I do in the Amazon is with indigenous pastors, some of whom live in these chronically flooded areas. Most of them and their families could move to drier and more sustainable areas, but in the words of my dear friend Pastor Cosme, "We stay in our villages because that's where our people are."

After a pause and with resolute conviction, Manoel continued, "But God always provides. At just the right time."

I sat with another couple, Pastor Manoel and his wife, Michele, who put it this way, "How can we simultaneously live where it's dry when our ministry is to people who live in flood conditions? It's simply not possible." After a pause and with resolute conviction, Manoel continued, "But God always provides. At just the right time."

Even when you can't understand the language, there's a glint in the eye of a good preacher, a certain compelling tone that lets you know when a story of God's faithfulness lies just beneath the surface. "Pastor, it sounds like you have a story behind that statement," I asserted.

"Indeed. There are many stories, but I will give you a special one."

I slid to the edge of my chair as he and Michele recounted a story about a particularly hot day out on the river when God did the unimaginable. Many years prior, when Manoel and Michele's four children were young, they found themselves in the throes of another rainy season. (There is no English term torrential enough for how soaked the Amazon gets during these months.) Their crops were long underwater and the fish had fled beneath the canopy of the jungle, making catching them next to impossible. On a steamy Sunday morning their family awoke to a pantry that was painfully bare. They'd never quite been down to nothing. "We can't take the family to church today," Michele told Manoel. "The kids' stomachs are growling. I need you to go fishing instead."

"He told me, 'The Lord will take care of us. I know it. We just need to be faithful.'"

Manoel insisted they get in their canoe and go to church as a family, believing that God would provide for their needs. Michele wasn't on board. (I do love a good pun.) "I wasn't happy with his decision," she recalled. "I wasn't worried about myself as for the little ones, the children. It's a tough thing to see your child hungry, asking for food. That's when it gets complicated. But I agreed to go to church with Manoel and we left in a small canoe, a little bitty thing holding the two of us and our four small children."

After the church service Manoel was asked if he could stay and help out with an additional service happening that afternoon. Manoel was torn, but still had a peace the Lord would somehow provide for his family. "I told the pastor I would help," he explained. "Michele looked at me with wide-open eyes."

At this point Michele jumped in and recounted her side of the story, "I couldn't believe him. I used to have a fiery temper and said what I felt in the moment without collecting my thoughts. We were both new believers in Jesus. But this time, I decided to trust Manoel's leading even though I wasn't happy about it. He told me, 'The Lord will take care of us. I know it. We just need to be faithful.'"

It was endearing to watch the two of them recount this story because all these years later, you can tell how much they love each other—how tender he is toward her and how radiantly she adores him. Through the lean and trying seasons, they help buoy one another's faith. Sometimes she's the one bolstering him when he's weak, and at other times he's the one reminding her, "God will provide."

After serving in the church on that scorching Sunday, Manoel and his family piled into their canoe and headed toward their home, obviously hungrier than when they'd left. "So you see," he explained, "we were in our tiny canoe heading home, when suddenly out of the water leapt an enormous fish that landed in our canoe! Right at Michele's feet. It was over three feet long!"

"It's funny how God does as he pleases," Michele said. "I think the Lord put it right at my feet because He wanted to see my reaction." Her laughter and passion were simply contagious as she unfolded the rest of the story. "The fish flopped around in the canoe, I flopped with it, trying to hold it while moving as little as possible, lest we capsize. What a mess. I finally secured it while Manoel kept urging me to hold on to the thing."

At this point in the story, I had to make sure I wasn't missing any details through the translator. After all, this was a fish story and fish stories are notorious for their exaggerated licenses. "So what you're telling me is that a fish jumped into your boat and you weren't fishing?"

"Right!" they both exclaimed. "We weren't fishing. We were just driving our canoe home and this enormous fish flew out of the water and landed in our boat." Michele continued, "I held it tight as Manoel steered until we got to my mother-in-law's home, where I cleaned it and fed the kids. It fed our family for a week!"

I was simultaneously laughing at the hilarity of it all and crying at the precision and tenderness of God. I'd never heard anything like it.

"What?" I exclaimed. "Who has a story like that?" Tears were running down my cheeks, my mascara had turned into black pools under my eyes (why I attempt to wear mascara in the jungle is another issue). I was simultaneously laughing at the hilarity of it all and crying at the precision and tenderness of God. I'd never heard anything like it. After pulling myself together, pen in hand and journal open, I asked them what kind of fish they'd caught—well, actually, I suppose I should say what kind of fish *jumped in their boat*. I wanted every last detail. "It was an arowana fish," Manoel replied, but didn't elaborate.

It wasn't until a few days later that Regina and I visited the fish market in Manaus and discovered that the arowana is a prized delicacy, and not cheap either. My Brazilian friend Francie describes it as the mother of all Amazon fish. Of course it is! I mean if God is going to go to all the trouble of sending dinner out of the water and into your boat, He might as well make it a filet mignon. I should have seen this coming.

Who needs farm-to-table when God can pull off river-to-canoe?

A friend of mine recently said, "If you've never experienced the wilderness you've never tasted manna." I suppose the same is true in the Amazon. If you've never been hungry and utterly dependent on the Lord, you've probably never had a God-fish fly into your boat.

I sat there in awe with Manoel and Michele, utterly marveling at the provision and timing of God. I wondered what a bite of fish straight from the Lord's hand tasted like. I wondered if they worshipped when they sat down to eat. I wondered if I would ever taste anything so glorious in all my life, or if I'd be willing to endure the sacrifices of what would be required to experience such a miracle. I dare say a bite of fish from the hand of God is unlike anything I've ever tasted. Who needs farm-to-table when God can pull off river-to-canoe?

The icing on the cake is when Manoel said, quite casually I might add, "This is not all that has happened, for even greater things the Lord has performed for us." Perhaps those stories will be for another cookbook. The following recipes in this section are inspired by trips to the Amazon, Regina's rich heritage from the south of Brazil, and both of our preeminent love for the people of the jungle who we've come to adore.

We've incorporated some of Regina's favorite dishes that easily translate into our American culture. (Note: there's no Brazilian pizza. You can thank me for the rest of your life.) As you cook these recipes and sit down to eat them, remember and pray for the countless image-bearers of God who are living in daily dependence on His provision in the Amazon jungle. Remember that we, too, live fully at the mercy of God, and that every meal we have on our plates is by His grace and from His hand. Whether we buy it from the store, grow it in our gardens, or it jumps straight into our canoe when we least expect it, our God provides, and He's always on time. ✺

Whole Grilled Fish
with Vinaigrette
(recipe on p. 148)

Greens and
Mango Salad with
Orange Dressing
(recipe on p. 149)

Black Bean Soup
(recipe on p. 150)

WHOLE GRILLED FISH WITH VINAIGRETTE

PREP TIME: 15 minutes (plus 1 hour for refrigeration) | **COOK TIME:** 20 minutes | **SERVES:** 4–6

VINAIGRETTE

2 cloves garlic, minced

5 Roma tomatoes, chopped

½ onion, chopped

1 ½ tablespoons olive oil

Juice from 1 lime

Salt and pepper, to taste

2 tablespoons chopped chives

2 tablespoons chopped parsley

FISH

1 fish (about 2 pounds whole red snapper or bass), cleaned and scaled

Olive oil or butter, for drizzling

Salt and pepper, to taste

2 lemons, sliced

Parsley sprigs

Tarragon sprigs

2 cloves garlic, minced

1 onion, sliced

1. **TO MAKE VINAIGRETTE:** Mix all ingredients and let it rest in the refrigerator for 1 hour.
2. Light an outdoor grill.
3. Brush the fish all over with olive oil, and season generously with salt and pepper inside and outside the fish. In the cavity, add some lemon slices, parsley, tarragon, garlic, and onion.
4. Generously spray a metal fish basket with cooking spray. Carefully place the fish on the basket, close, and put on the grill. Drizzle with olive oil or butter. Grill about 10 minutes on medium-high heat. Turn the basket over and grill for another 10 minutes.
5. Set the fish on a platter and let stand for 5 minutes before serving. Drizzle with more olive oil, and serve with vinaigrette.

Ⓡ

In the Amazon, river fish are a daily, staple meal. On our mission trips, our cook loves to serve tambaqui grilled with molho vinaigrette—a vinaigrette dressing similar to pico de gallo. Tambaqui is a very mild fish with white flesh. It can grow up to 3 ½ feet long and be 97 pounds. We had a chance to see them in person at the fish market in Manaus, and we assure you, it is a big fish! Though we cannot find this particular fish in America, we can substitute with any other whole fish of your preference. It is a very simple recipe.

❖ *Pictured on page 146*

GREENS AND MANGO SALAD WITH ORANGE DRESSING

PREP TIME: 20 minutes | **COOK TIME:** 0 minutes | **SERVES:** 4–6

ORANGE DRESSING

¾ cup vegetable oil

1 tablespoon sugar

1 clove garlic, minced

Salt and pepper, to taste

4 tablespoons red wine vinegar

1 orange, juiced, keeping orange pieces

SALAD

4 cups mixed greens of your choice

2 mangoes, peeled and sliced

2 tablespoons toasted walnuts

1. **TO MAKE DRESSING:** Mix vegetable oil, sugar, garlic, salt, pepper, and vinegar, whisking well to combine. Add oranges and orange juice. Keep in the refrigerator.
2. Arrange the greens on a platter, and add mango slices on top. Top with orange dressing and toasted walnuts.

Pictured on page 147 ❖

BLACK BEAN SOUP

PREP TIME: 10 minutes (plus overnight soaking) | **COOK TIME:** 2 hours | **SERVES:** 4–6

2 cups dry black beans

2 tablespoons vegetable oil

1 cup onion, chopped

2 cloves garlic, minced

½ cup carrots, cut into very small pieces

Salt and pepper, to taste

2 quarts water

Sour cream

Chopped chives or cilantro

1. In a large bowl, add the beans and cover with water. Let soak overnight.

2. In a large soup pot, heat the vegetable oil over medium-high heat. Add the onion and garlic and cook until tender. Then add the carrots and cook for about 5 minutes.

3. Drain the beans and add to the pot. Salt and pepper, to taste.

4. Add 2 quarts of water and let cook until beans are tender (about 1 1/2 hours). Add more water if needed.

5. Puree everything in the soup pot with an immersion blender, or transfer contents into a blender and then return to pot. (Add water if it is too thick.)

6. Serve hot with a dollop of sour cream and sprinkle with chives or cilantro.

❖ *Pictured on page 147*

BRAZILIAN CHICKEN SALAD

PREP TIME: 20 minutes | **COOK TIME:** 20 minutes | **SERVES:** 4–6

3 chicken breasts, shredded (or use store-bought roasted chicken)

2 tablespoons extra virgin olive oil

2 cloves garlic, minced

1 medium onion, diced

Salt and pepper, to taste

2 tablespoons parsley, finely chopped

2 tablespoons chives, chopped

1 medium apple, julienned

1 pound carrots, julienned

1 cup green beans, blanched

½ cup celery, finely julienned

½ cup orange or red bell pepper, blanched

1 cup Duke's mayonnaise (or your favorite mayonnaise)

1 ½ cups sour cream

1 large can shoestring potatoes

1. In a large pot over medium heat, brown chicken breasts in extra virgin olive oil, about 10 minutes per side. Add the garlic and onion, and sauté for another minute. Add salt and pepper, to taste. Once the chicken is cooked, let it cool and then shred the meat.

2. In a large bowl, combine the chicken with the remaining herbs and vegetables. Add the mayonnaise and sour cream and toss the salad until well coated. Serve chilled with shoestring potatoes on the side.

This is a crisp and savory chicken salad, known as Salpicão de Frango in Brazil, served with crunchy shoestring potatoes. It's a great way to enjoy a plateful of colorful vegetables! Buy a roasted chicken from your local grocer to save time, and add the shoestring potatoes right at the end to make sure they don't lose their crunch.

Bife á Milanesa
(Steak Parmigiana)
(recipe on p. 156)

154

Pork Ribs with Parmesan (recipe on p. 157)

BIFE Á MILANESA (STEAK PARMIGIANA)

PREP: 30 minutes | **COOK TIME:** 1 hour 30 minutes | **SERVES:** 6

SAUCE

1 medium onion, chopped

1 tablespoon olive oil

1 green bell pepper, seeded and diced

1 large clove garlic, crushed

2 pounds Roma tomatoes, seeded, peeled, and diced

1 tablespoon sugar

Salt and pepper, to taste

1 tablespoon butter

2 large basil leafs, julienned

STEAK

3 pounds sirloin steaks, thinly sliced

Salt and pepper, to taste

1 ½ cups all purpose flour, for dredging

5 eggs

2–3 cups bread crumbs, plain

3 tablespoons canola oil

12–15 slices Provolone cheese

1. **TO MAKE SAUCE:** Using a sauce pan, sauté the onion in olive oil until translucent over medium-high heat. Add the green bell pepper and sauté for another 5 minutes until the pepper is slightly tender.

2. Add garlic, tomatoes, sugar, salt, and pepper, and let cook for about an hour over medium heat.

3. When ready, add one tablespoon of butter and the julienned basil leaves. Set aside.

4. **TO MAKE STEAKS:** Season the steaks with salt and pepper, to taste. Place the steaks between plastic wrap or wax paper and pound to tenderize. (Legend has it that restaurants would pound the beef into almost translucent sheets to make them larger and more tender.)

5. In three bowls or plastic containers, set up the flour, eggs, and bread crumbs.

6. To bread the beef, start by dredging the steaks in flour and shaking off the excess. Next dip them into the whisked egg, allowing the excess wash to drip off before finally placing the steaks in the bread crumbs. Press the bread crumbs into the meat and pile the steaks on a plate.

7. On high heat, fry the steaks in canola oil until golden brown. Set them on a tray over paper towels to drain, and cover with half a slice of Provolone cheese while still warm. Pour the homemade tomato sauce over the steaks and serve with rice.

No matter the man in our extended family—it could be my husband or son-in-law—Bife á Milanesa is always requested for ordinary days and special days alike! It was also a favorite of my father's for many years.

❖ *Pictured on page 154*

PORK RIBS WITH PARMESAN

PREP TIME: 45 minutes (plus 1 hour for refrigeration) **|** **COOK TIME:** 20–30 minutes **|** **SERVES:** 4–6

2 cloves garlic, minced

1 small onion, chopped

2 tablespoons lime juice

2 tablespoons olive oil

½ teaspoon salt

½ teaspoon pepper

2 pounds baby back ribs, cut in individual ribs

1 cup Parmesan cheese, grated

1 cup panko bread crumbs

1. Preheat oven to 350 degrees.

2. In a small bowl, mix garlic, onion, lime juice, olive oil, salt, and pepper, and rub the ribs (cut individual) very well. Cover and refrigerate for 1 hour.

3. Mix the Parmesan cheese and panko bread crumbs in a bowl and drench each rib in it. Arrange the ribs on a baking dish and bake for 20–30 minutes or until tender and crispy.

Pictured on page 155 ❖

Rice
(recipe on p. 159)

"Farofa"
(recipe on p. 160)

Brazilian Feijoada
(Black Bean Stew)
American Style
(recipe on p. 159)

Zozo's Hot
Pepper Sauce
(recipe on p. 161)

Stir-Fried Kale
with Bacon
(recipe on p. 160)

BRAZILIAN FEIJOADA (BLACK BEAN STEW) AMERICAN STYLE

PREP TIME: 20 minutes (plus overnight soaking) | **COOK TIME:** 2 hours | **SERVES:** 6–8

STEW

- 2 cups dry black beans
- 2 tablespoons olive oil
- 4 slices bacon, cut into small pieces
- 1 cup onion, chopped
- 4 large cloves garlic, minced

- 1 bay leaf
- Salt and pepper, to taste
- 1 package kielbasa sausage, cut into cubes
- 1 pound boneless smoked pork chops, cut into cubes

- 2 smoked ham hocks
- ½ cup green onion, chopped
- Orange slices
- **Optional:** Hot pepper, to taste

1. Place dry beans in a large bowl and cover with water. Soak overnight.
2. The next day, drain the black beans and place in a large saucepan, cover with water, and cook for about 30 minutes.
3. In a large skillet with 1 tablespoon of olive oil, fry the pieces of bacon until crispy. Add onions and garlic, sauté about 4 minutes. Drop the mixture over the beans. Add the bay leaf, salt, and pepper.
4. Add the meats to the beans and cook until beans are soft.
5. Remove ham hocks from the beans, cut off the meat and discard the rest. Cut meat into cubes and return to the pot.
6. Before serving, sprinkle with green onions.
7. Add meat stew on top of the rice, and serve with orange slices, stir-fried kale, and *farofa* (see p. 160).

RICE

- 2 tablespoons vegetable oil
- ¼ onion, diced

- ½ clove garlic, minced
- 2 cups white long rice

- 4 cups boiling water
- Salt

1. Heat vegetable oil in a saucepan over medium-low heat. Add onion and garlic; cook and stir until softened. Add rice and fry for about 3 minutes. Stir in boiling water and salt.
2. Reduce heat, cover, and cook until rice is tender, 20–30 minutes.

STIR-FRIED KALE WITH BACON

2 bunches kale, washed and
stems removed

3 slices bacon, cut very thin

1 tablespoon olive oil

1 clove garlic, minced

Salt and pepper, to taste

1. Cut the kale julienne, very thin.
2. In a skillet, fry the pieces of bacon until crispy. Add olive oil, and let it warm up. Then add the garlic and kale and stir-fry on medium-high heat, stirring constantly for about 10 minutes. The kale will greatly reduce after cooking. Add salt and pepper, to taste.

FAROFA

4 tablespoons butter

1 clove garlic, minced

2 cups "farinha de mandioca"
(cassava flour)

Salt and pepper, to taste

1. In a small saucepan, melt the butter until lightly browned, add the garlic and sauté for just a minute. Add the flour and stir constantly, being careful not to burn. Add salt and pepper, to taste.

Ⓡ Feijoada *is a delicious stew of meats and black beans that's traditionally served over rice with fresh orange slices, stir-fried kale, and farofa (cassava flour toasted with butter garlic and salt). Though the original recipe calls for all parts of the pig, we have adapted to ingredients found in American grocery stores.*

❖ Pictured on page 158

ZOZO'S HOT PEPPER SAUCE

PREP TIME: 20 minutes | **COOK TIME:** rest uncovered 2 hours; refrigerate 2 days | **SERVES:** 6–8

1 pound peppers (fresh habañeros, chilies, cayennes, or any other hot pepper)

3 cloves garlic

1 large onion, cut in quarters

2 tablespoons red wine vinegar

½ cup chives, chopped

½ cup parsley, chopped

Salt and pepper, to taste

½ cup olive oil

1. Add all ingredients except olive oil into food processor, and process until very fine sauce.
2. Pour sauce into a glass jar and top with olive oil, about 1/2 inch over the sauce. Let it rest uncovered for about 2 hours.
3. Close the jar tightly and keep in the refrigerator. After 2 days it is ready to use.

This is my father's patented hot sauce recipe. I used to sell it in Brazil at the local farmer's market. Add to any recipe to spice up the flavor!

®

Pictured on page 158 ❖

Vilma's Flan
(recipe on p. 164)

Mousse De Maracujá
(Passion Fruit Mousse)
(recipe on p. 165)

Brigadeiro—
Brazilian Traditional Dessert
(recipe on p. 166)

163

VILMA'S FLAN

PREP TIME: 15 minutes | **COOK TIME:** 2 hours | **SERVES:** 16

1 ½ cups sugar

2 cups water

1 (14 ounce) can sweetened
condensed milk

1 ½ cups whole milk

5 eggs

½ teaspoon vanilla

1. Preheat oven to 350 degrees.

2. In a small saucepan over medium heat, melt the sugar in the water, stirring constantly until it reaches the consistency and color of an amber caramel.

3. Pour the sauce into an 8-inch round pudding pan (one designed to pair with a bain-marie). If you can't find this type of pan, individual ramekins work just as well. Turn the pan as you pour the caramel, in order to completely coat the bottom and sides.

4. Mix all the remaining ingredients in a blender until well combined. Pour the mixture over the caramel-coated pan. Cover and bake in a water bath for 45 minutes–1 hour, or until the pudding is firm.

5. If using ramekins, divide the mixture equally among the bowls, set them in a baking pan and fill with hot water to within 1 inch of the top of the ramekins. Allow the flan to cool completely in the fridge.

TIP: When ready to serve, place the pan in a hot water bath for about 3 minutes to loosen the caramel. With the ramekins, run a knife around the outside edge to loosen. When the flan feels free from the pan, place a plate over the top and flip. It should come down to the plate with all the caramel sauce . . . delicious!

R *This recipe is a classic in our family. A favorite of my husband, and it's now become one of my family's most requested desserts.*

❖ *Pictured on page 162*   164

MOUSSE DE MARACUJÁ (PASSION FRUIT MOUSSE)

PREP TIME: 10 minutes | **COOK TIME:** refrigerate approximately 2 hours | **SERVES:** 4–6

1 (14 ounce) can sweetened condensed milk

1 (14 ounce) can table cream

1 ½ cans juice from passion fruit (measure in the sweetened condensed milk can)

1. Beat all ingredients in blender until well-mixed.
2. Transfer to a bowl and refrigerate until firm.
3. Take out and place in serving bowl or in individual ramekins. Decorate with the pulp of fresh passion fruit.

Pictured on page 163 ❖

BRIGADEIRO— BRAZILIAN TRADITIONAL DESSERT

PREP TIME: 15 minutes | **COOK TIME:** 10–15 minutes (plus 1 hour for cooling) | **SERVES:** 18

CHOCOLATE VERSION

1 (14 ounce) can sweetened condensed milk

3 tablespoons powdered cocoa

2 tablespoons butter, unsalted

Chocolate sprinkles for rolling

1. Combine sweetened condensed milk, cocoa, and butter in a saucepan; bring to a boil. Reduce heat to low and cook, stirring constantly, until brigadeiro mixture thickens and pulls away from the bottom and sides when the pan is tilted, 10–15 minutes.
2. Remove from heat and let brigadeiro mixture cool to room temperature, about 1 hour.
3. Scoop teaspoonfuls of the brigadeiro mixture and roll into balls with greased hands.
4. Spread chocolate sprinkles on a shallow plate. Dip and roll brigadeiros in sprinkles.

COCONUT VERSION: BRIGADEIRO DE COCO

1 (14 ounce) can sweetened condensed milk

7 ounces coconut, shredded and unsweetened

1 egg yolk

2 tablespoons butter, unsalted

Crystal sugar for rolling

1. Combine sweetened condensed milk, coconut, egg yolk, and butter in a saucepan; bring to a boil. Reduce heat to low and cook, stirring constantly, until coconut brigadeiro mixture thickens and pulls away from the bottom and sides when the pan is tilted, 10–15 minutes.
2. Remove from heat and let coconut brigadeiro mixture cool to room temperature, about 1 hour.
3. Scoop teaspoonfuls of the coconut brigadeiro mixture and roll into balls with greased hands.
4. Spread crystal sugar on a shallow plate. Dip and roll coconut brigadeiros in sugar.

❖ *Pictured on page 163*

BREAKFAST
AND THE ART
OF INVITATION

For me, cooking has always been about community. I realize this isn't the case for everyone. I know a few people who are just as happy to cook for themselves as they are for a group of people. I respect this, but I am not that person.

It's kind of like the old adage: if a tree falls in the forest and no one's there to hear it, did it make a sound? Except mine is: if you make a meal in your kitchen and no one's there to eat it, why didn't you just pour yourself a bowl of cereal and go to bed? I know, I know: this could be symptomatic of deeper issues in my life. Or maybe I've just always seen eating as needing the additional component of community for a meal to really come alive.

Now I don't necessarily need anyone around *while* I'm cooking. You've never seen a happier, all-by-herself, dicer of carrots, celery, and onion than I am on a Saturday afternoon—just as long as I know someone is eventually coming. This is all about expectation. Every stir of a spoon or stroke of a knife is in anticipation of those who will soon be bustling through the front door and emptying straight into my kitchen. If the end game entails a table full of people, a couple friends at my kitchen island, or even just one other person, cooking alone doesn't equate to lonely while cooking.

The unspoken expectation is that if you see someone who looks lonely at church, you have a guest staying with you, you run into your neighbor who has no plans, or your hamster looks sad, he or she is welcome to come.

Thankfully, my friends share this desire for cooking and eating together. It's one of our favorite activities. We try to be mindful of extending invitations, often last-minute casual ones, to those who could use a good meal and some conversation. My friend April is a natural at the open-armed invitation. "The more the merrier" is her motto. And in some cases, the stranger the merrier. (If you've ever been invited to her house, don't read into this.)

Every so often, April makes an elaborate Sunday brunch we like to call *April's Breakfast Wagon*, or *ABW* for short. I think we came up with that name on a day we were urging her to open her own breakfast diner. It was a very exciting prospect for everyone except her. The idea was short-lived but the name caught on.

When April decides—usually on the night beforehand—that she's having an ABW, she alerts her friends and in-town family. Once you've received her invitation, the unspoken expectation is that if you see someone who looks lonely at church, you have a guest staying with you, you run into your neighbor who has no plans, or your hamster looks sad, he or she is welcome to come. You don't even have to tell April in advance that you're bringing someone extra. She always has enough sweet potato hash browns, fried eggs, kolaches, and coffee to go around. An extra place setting is always waiting in the wings.

This approach actually stresses me out a bit, but I'm also about as flexible as a two-by-four. I love cooking casually for close friends and family, but if the guest list expands beyond that I can get a little frenetic. April has helped me learn to relax, to make a little extra, and to keep the ingredients quality but unfussy. In Ida Garten's cookbook *Cooking for Jeffrey*, she framed it this way: "Instead of the elaborate food I used to cook for dinner parties, I learned that people wanted simple food at home."* April innately understands this. She's always reminding me: *Don't stress. Grab an extra chair. Give your guests an inviting hug. Put a well-crafted pancake and a sausage patty in front of them and let them know they're loved and welcome in your home. You don't have to complicate this.*

Another lesson I've learned is this: if inviting people over stresses you out, cook what you know. My friend, Mary Katharine (who we call MK), is great with a grill. Summers in particular are a delight on her screened-in cedar porch. Rotisserie chickens, rib eyes, mahi mahi, chicken legs, grilled vegetables—those are the smells and images that come to mind when I think about gatherings on her porch, with those vaulted ceilings and a tin roof. (The setting is so comfortable and her hospitality so inviting that when my parents come to visit—my own flesh and blood, please keep in mind—they've been known to stay at her house instead of mine. I don't know what to do about this except to build my own porch.) While MK is a bit less spontaneous than April and I, she can still easily accommodate last-minute guests because she's comfortable grilling. What's a few more chicken legs on the grill when you know what you're doing?

While April's *modus operandi* is: how about we roast a leg of lamb in the next two hours and invite a surprise number of guests over, MK likes a wee bit more structure—typically the kind that includes a select number of people and a set menu. Then again, MK is the executive director of Justice & Mercy International and executive directors aren't known for their whimsy. April, on the other hand, is a video producer who drives a powder blue Vespa scooter—they are strikingly different humans who wear different hospitality aprons.

I, perhaps, fall someplace in the middle of these two. I'm not a great planner and I'm also not terribly spontaneous, putting me someplace in the category of frustrating for people. I contend that this is why I love serving soup so much. It's contained and predictable but can also serve pretty much any number of extras who may be dropping by.

As we consider the different personalities and contributions when it comes to hosting, we can't leave out the non-cooks who are happy to pick up the items you forgot to buy at the grocery store, clean the dishes after the meal, and entertain guests with lively conversation while you're running around in the kitchen with your hair in flames. This is my friend Paige. She's always there for you in a pinch, just don't ask her to make anything. You can't have too many of these kinds of friends or relatives when it comes to entertaining. If I could summarize my quirky cooking world, April serves up world-class brunches and Mary Katharine can grill you into the next Fourth of July. Paige brings an enormously fun personality and a happy willingness to clean dishes. My contribution is that I make tomato-based pasta dishes, soup with homemade broth, and grow my own asparagus. It takes all kinds. What I'm grateful for is that we all have two things in common: a love for good food and a desire to be inclusive.

We all have two things in common: a love for good food and a desire to be inclusive.

I've had enough experiences where I've either felt left out of a group of people, or found myself part of the "inside" group while others were left out. At some point in my life, I realized I didn't want to ever be part of this latter group. The Lord encouraged me to open my doors, reach out, and welcome people in. I made a conscious decision that whether it was morning coffee and muffins on the porch, or tortilla soup around a football game, if my friends or I knew of someone who could use an invitation to eat and enjoy community, well then, a place at the table would be made. I can't say that I'm always excited about making unexpected last-minute provisions, or that I don't have to adjust my attitude at times. But all of us try to support each other when it comes to opening up our homes and tables to anyone who needs the warm embrace of a meal.

I also try to keep in mind opportunities to cook for people who aren't in my immediate circle— to invite people over who may not be able to give back in any way. When we are used to only inviting over "our people," this requires intention. In Luke 14:12–14, Luke tells a compelling story about Jesus sitting around a dinner table with the Pharisees (Jewish religious leaders of the day). He noticed that they were taking the best and most prominent seats at the table. After discouraging this practice, Jesus took His instruction further. He told them that the next time they threw a dinner party they were to specifically invite people who couldn't return the favor, those who didn't run in their circles. Put on a spread for the sick, the hurting, those on the fringes of society. Those who had nothing to give in return.

For us today this may also include welcoming the loud talker, the somewhat awkward, or the quintessential Debbie Downer. I know what you're thinking: this can really wreck a brunch. But I believe that Jesus meant what He said, and expects His people to follow His instruction both in His own time period and in ours.

Of course, this doesn't mean that we should never invite over our loved ones, or those we know we're going to laugh and carry on with late into the night. Oh, the meals that Jesus had with His *friends*. The gift of friendship and fellowship is one of God's greatest gifts to us, and we should joyfully foster and savor it. But we can't forget those who are often passed over, who no one stops to take notice of, who don't have a home to be welcomed into for a homemade meal. I really do believe that He blesses this kind of cooking.

The gift of friendship and fellowship is one of God's greatest gifts to us, and we should joyfully foster and savor it.

I wanted to include a breakfast section, because brunch has been such a special time of gathering for me. If it's an ABW, it's typically after church, naturally giving rise to lively discussions about the sermons we heard that morning and how those truths intersect with our lives. Will and Harper love twirling on April's vintage chartreuse bar stools whilst downing kolaches and eggs, no doubt absorbing what it means to eat in community and to always have a place setting for someone who may need it. I don't know what your cooking specialty is, but never underestimate the blessing of a home-cooked meal for someone who could really use one. Whether you drive a scooter, run a business, are great with a chicken soup, or don't cook at all but know how to be fun, someone needs what you bring to the table. ✀

* Ida Garten, *Cooking for Jeffrey* (New York: Clarkson Potter, 2016), 133.

*Kristin's Swedish
Granola
(recipe on p. 178)*

*Overnight Oats
(recipe on p. 179)*

Fresh Strawberry Muffins
(recipe on p. 180)

177

KRISTIN'S SWEDISH GRANOLA

PREP TIME: 35 minutes | **COOK TIME:** 1 hour | **SERVES:** 12 or more

6 cups oats (regular, not quick oats)

⅓ cup wheat germ

½ cup sunflower seeds

1 cup almonds, slivered

½ cup almonds, whole

¼ cup brown sugar

½ teaspoon salt

½ cup raw coconut chips

½ cup honey

⅓ cup water

½ cup vegetable oil

2 teaspoons vanilla

1. Preheat oven to 335 degrees.
2. Combine first 8 ingredients in a large bowl.
3. Combine honey, water, vegetable oil, and vanilla in a separate small bowl and stir into dry ingredients, adding more honey if needed.
4. Grease two 9 x 13-inch pans. Bake granola mixture approximately 1 hour, stirring every 15 minutes. (Watch closely at the end!)
5. Cool completely and store in an airtight container.

K

This is a fabulous granola recipe you can serve over Greek yogurt. Top with honey and fresh berries if desired.

❖ *Pictured on page 176*

OVERNIGHT OATS

PREP TIME: 30 minutes | **COOK TIME:** 0 minutes | **SERVES:** 4

2 cups quick oats

2 ¼ cups almond milk

2 tablespoons chia seeds

1 tablespoon flax seeds

3 tablespoons peanut butter, softened

2 tablespoons honey

1 tablespoon agave

1 banana, sliced

½ cup pecans or peanuts, toasted and chopped

Optional: 3 tablespoons cocoa powder and chocolate chips, to taste

1. Place oats, almond milk, chia seeds, flax seeds, peanut butter, honey, and agave in a bowl and mix well. Divide in 4 cups or jars. Place in refrigerator and let sit overnight.

2. Take out of refrigerator and serve cold. Top with banana slices (or other fruit of your choice), pecans, or peanuts.

NOTE: To make a chocolate recipe, add 3 tablespoons of cocoa powder and some chocolate chips.

Pictured on page 176 ❖

FRESH STRAWBERRY MUFFINS

PREP TIME: 30 minutes | **COOK TIME:** 25–35 minutes | **SERVES:** 12

2 cups flour

¼ teaspoon salt

1 tablespoon baking powder

1 cup sugar

1 cup sour cream

4 tablespoons butter, melted

1 large egg

1 cup strawberries, washed and dried, cut into cubes

Optional: You can also substitute blueberries or bananas for the strawberries.

1. Preheat oven to 350 degrees.
2. In a mixing bowl, combine flour, salt, and baking powder; stir to blend.
3. In another bowl, mix sugar and sour cream, stirring until blended well. Add melted butter and stir. Then add egg and stir until all is combined.
4. Toss the strawberries into the flour mixture, and gently stir until combined. Add the sugar mixture to the flour mixture with just a few strokes to fold it all together.
5. Butter or spray 12 muffin cups. (You can also use muffin liners.)
6. Spoon equal portions into each prepared muffin cup.
7. Bake the muffins for about 25–35 minutes, or until muffins are golden brown and an inserted toothpick comes out clean.

K

This is essentially a cupcake, but I feel so much better calling it a muffin. I really love this recipe because the sour cream keeps the muffins from being dry or crumbly. You can make these in any season, substituting strawberries for seasonal fruits.

❖ *Pictured on page 177*

APRIL'S SWEET POTATO, KALE, AND EGG BOWL

PREP TIME: 40 minutes | **COOK TIME:** 30–40 minutes | **SERVES:** 4–6

4–5 large sweet potatoes, cut in cubes

1 tablespoon olive oil

Paprika, sprinkle

Salt and pepper, to taste

1 pound pork sausage, cooked

1 pound bacon

2–3 pounds kale or spinach, washed

12 eggs

2–3 avocados, peeled, pitted, and sliced

1. Preheat oven to 375 degrees.
2. In a large bowl, toss the sweet potatoes with olive oil, sprinkle with paprika, salt, and pepper. Add cooked sausage and mix well. Lay the mixture on a baking sheet and bake for 30–40 minutes, turning the mixture occasionally. Be careful not to make them too crisp.
3. When potato mixture has been in the oven for 10 minutes, take another baking sheet and lay out the bacon flat, and bake for 20 minutes.
4. In a medium skillet, sauté the kale or spinach with 1 teaspoon of olive oil very fast, 3–4 minutes.
5. When everything is almost done, start the eggs. The eggs can be fried, poached, or scrambled.
6. Scoop a generous portion of the sweet potato mixture into a nice serving bowl. Add eggs, then 2 pieces of crispy bacon, and finish with a nice spoon of kale or spinach. Top with slices of avocado.

This is a Sunday brunch favorite. My friend April serves this dish in individual bowls. This protein-rich meal is also great served alongside sweeter goods like pancakes, kolaches, or donuts.

Mexican Breakfast Burrito
(recipe on p. 186)

Sun-Dried Tomato and
Goat Cheese Frittata
(recipe on p. 187)

185

MEXICAN BREAKFAST BURRITO

PREP TIME: 25 minutes (plus 5 hours for refrigeration) | **COOK TIME:** 15 minutes | **SERVES:** 4

SALSA

2 cloves garlic, minced

5 Roma tomatoes, chopped

2 red bell peppers, seeded and cut in small pieces

2 jalapeños, seeded and chopped

½ onion, chopped

1 ½ tablespoons olive oil

Juice from 1 lime

Chili powder, to taste

Salt and pepper, to taste

Chopped chives, cilantro, or parsley to taste

BURRITO

8 ounces chorizo or other sausage

1 teaspooon olive oil

8 eggs

1 tablespoon heavy cream

Salt and pepper, to taste

2 tablespoons butter

4 flour tortillas

1 cup Monterey Jack cheese, shredded

1 large avocado, peeled, pitted, and sliced

Optional: 1 tablespoon chives, chopped

1. **TO MAKE SALSA:** Mix all ingredients and let it rest in the refrigerator for 5 hours.
2. **TO MAKE BURRITO:** Cook the chorizo or sausage in a skillet with olive oil over medium-high heat, stirring and breaking it up until cooked through. Remove from heat and cover to keep warm.
3. Whisk together eggs, heavy cream, salt, and pepper. Melt the butter in a skillet; add the eggs and cook, stirring to scramble until just cooked through. Remove from heat.
4. Place tortillas on large sheet of parchment paper. Spoon one fourth of each: the chorizo or sausage, eggs, Monterey Jack cheese, avocados, and salsa to taste. Fold bottom of the tortilla over most of the filling, then fold over sides overlapping them. Wrap a small sheet of parchment paper around the burrito, and tie a colorful string around it. Serve hot.

❖ *Pictured on page 184*

SUN-DRIED TOMATO AND GOAT CHEESE FRITTATA

PREP TIME: 10 minutes | **COOK TIME:** 20 minutes | **SERVES:** 4–6

6 eggs

1 cup milk

Salt and pepper, to taste

4 ounces Goat cheese, broken into large chunks

¼ cup olive oil, plus more for drizzling

2 cloves garlic, minced

1 ½ cups sun-dried tomatoes

4 cups arugula, roughly chopped and divided

1. Preheat oven to 375 degrees.

2. In a large bowl, whisk together eggs and milk until smooth. Season with salt and pepper, to taste. Add Goat cheese and stir just enough to coat. Set sauce aside.

3. Heat 1/4 cup olive oil in a large oven-proof skillet over medium heat. Add garlic and sauce, about 1 minute. Add sun-dried tomatoes and 3 1/2 cups of arugula, stirring for 1 minute.

4. Pour egg mixture over the ingredients in the pan and cook about 5 minutes or until the eggs begin to set.

5. Transfer the skillet to the preheated oven and bake about 10–15 minutes, or until frittata has set and is slightly golden on top. Remove from oven and let stand for 5 minutes. Sprinkle the frittata with the remaining 1/2 cup arugula leaves and drizzle with olive oil. Slice into wedges and serve.

Pictured on page 185 ❖

CREPES PARTY

PREP TIME: 30 minutes (plus 30 minutes for refrigeration) | **COOK TIME:** 20 minutes | **SERVES:** 6–8

CREPES

6 tablespoons butter, unsalted

1 ½ cups flour

1 tablespoon sugar

¼ teaspoon salt

4 large eggs

1 ½ cups milk, more if needed

FILLING AND TOPPING IDEAS

Apples, sliced thin with Brie cheese slices

Chocolate ganache with whipping cream and sliced strawberries

Hazelnut spread with hazelnut pieces and whipping cream

Banana, chocolate ganache

Banana, hazelnut

Peaches and whipped cream

Sautéed spinach with garlic and olive oil and shredded cheese with béchamel sauce

Ham and cheese slices

Spinach, chicken, and Goat cheese

Confectioner's powdered sugar, chocolate glaze, or herbs to decorate

1. Melt the butter in the microwave for 1 minute and set aside.

2. In a large bowl add the flour, sugar, and salt. Make a well in the center of the flour mixture and add the eggs. Whisk well until mixed. Pour half of the milk into the eggs and whisk constantly to prevent lumps; continue adding the rest of the milk. Mix all until it makes a smooth batter. Gradually add the butter. At this point, the batter will be the consistency of a thin cream. Cover and let refrigerate for 30 minutes.

3. Heat the crepe pan and drop a small piece of butter to coat the pan (only necessary for the first crepe). With a ladle, drop about 3 tablespoons of the batter (you may need more if the pan is larger). Do not add too much batter or the crepe will be too thick.

4. Using an offset spatula, spread the batter around. Fry crepe over medium heat until it is set on top and brown underneath, about 1 minute. Carefully loosen the edges with the spatula and turn the crepe over. Let it fry until it's brown on the other side. At this point, slide the crepe onto a platter and keep making them until the batter is finished.

5. Use the pile of crepes immediately for party purposes or freeze for future use.

6. If having a crepes party, display your choice filling and topping ingredients for guests and allow them to make their own creation.

Aunt Elotia's
Blueberry Buckle
(recipe on p. 193)

Orange Knots
(recipe on p. 192)

190

*Peach Bread Pudding
with Crème Anglaise
(recipe on p. 194)*

ORANGE KNOTS

PREP TIME: 1 hour 40 minutes (including rising time) | **COOK TIME:** 15 minutes | **SERVES:** 8–10

KNOTS

6 ½ cups flour

1 package yeast

1 ¼ cups milk, warm

½ cup butter

2 eggs

⅓ cup sugar

Salt, pinch

½ can sweetened condensed milk

2 tablespoons orange zest

¼ cup orange juice

ICING

1 ½ cups confectioner's powdered sugar

1 ½ teaspoons orange zest

½ cup orange juice

1. Mix 5 1/2 cups of flour and yeast in a large bowl. Warm the milk and butter to about 120 degrees, and add to the flour mixture. Add the eggs and beat in an electric mixer fitted with a paddle attachment for about 4 minutes. Mix in the sugar, salt, sweetened condensed milk, orange zest and the juice. Add the extra flour if needed to form the dough. Knead the dough out until soft and elastic.

2. Shape the dough into a ball, cover, and let it rise until it doubles in size.

3. Preheat oven to 350 degrees.

4. Divide the dough in half and roll each portion into a 12 x 7-inch rectangle. Cut the rectangle in half and into strips, about 7 inches long x 2 inches wide. Tie the strips loosely into a knot.

5. Place the knots on a baking sheet lined with parchment paper. Cover and let rise until doubled in size.

6. Bake for 12–15 minutes or until lightly golden on top. Remove from oven and cool on a wire rack.

7. **TO MAKE ICING:** In a small bowl, combine the confectioner's powdered sugar, orange zest, and orange juice to form a glaze. Drizzle the glaze over the orange knots when warm, and you're ready to serve.

These soft and sweet rolls are perfect for an autumn brunch. With just a hint of orange baked in, and a gorgeous orange glaze to top them off, you will have a hard time making them last!

AUNT ELOTIA'S BLUEBERRY BUCKLE

PREP TIME: 25 minutes | **COOK TIME:** 25–35 minutes | **SERVES:** 6–8

DOUGH

¾ cup sugar

¼ cup shortening, softened

1 egg

½ cup milk

2 cups flour

1 teaspoon baking powder

½ teaspoon salt

2 cups blueberries, well-drained

CRUMB MIXTURE

½ cup sugar

⅓ cup flour

½ teaspoon cinnamon

¼ cup butter, softened

1. Preheat oven to 350 degrees.
2. **TO MAKE DOUGH:** Mix all dough ingredients except the blueberries together in large bowl. Once well-mixed, fold in blueberries. Pour mixture into greased and floured 8 x 8-inch pan.
3. **TO MAKE CRUMB MIXTURE:** Mix all crumb mixture ingredients together and sprinkle on top of dough. Bake for 25–35 minutes and serve warm.

I found this recipe handwritten on a notecard in an old cabin. My friend's Aunt Elotia was known for making this with fresh Michigan blueberries in the summer. Don't be afraid of the shortening. Sometimes you have to go for it when making a breakfast cake.

K

Pictured on page 190 ❖

PEACH BREAD PUDDING WITH CRÈME ANGLAISE

PREP TIME: 45 minutes (plus 2 hours refrigeration) | **COOK TIME:** 40–45 minutes | **SERVES:** 8–10

BREAD PUDDING

12 slices brioche bread, cut into 1-inch cubes

2 ½ cups fresh peaches, peeled and chopped

½ package cream cheese (4 ounce), softened, cut in small pieces

1 cup pecans, toasted and chopped

2 cups whole milk

8 eggs, lightly beaten

1 ½ cup heavy cream

¾ cup sugar

½ teaspoon vanilla paste (or vanilla extract)

½ teaspoon sea salt

¼ teaspoon nutmeg

½ teaspoon cinnamon

CRÈME ANGLAISE

2 cups whole milk

¼ cup sugar

½ teaspoon vanilla paste (or vanilla extract)

4 egg yolks

1. Grease a rectangular baking dish.

2. In a large bowl, combine the pieces of bread, peaches, small pieces of cream cheese, and pecans. Mix all together and drop into the baking dish.

3. In another bowl, mix the milk, eggs, heavy cream, sugar, vanilla, sea salt, nutmeg, and cinnamon. Mix well and put over the bread mixture. Using the back of a spoon, press down to moisten all the ingredients. Cover and let stand in the refrigerator for about 2 hours.

4. Preheat oven to 350 degrees, and bake the bread pudding uncovered for 40–45 minutes or until set.

5. Serve with warm crème anglaise.

6. **TO MAKE CRÈME ANGLAISE:** In a heavy saucepan bring milk, 2 tablespoons sugar, and vanilla to a boil over medium heat.

7. In a large bowl, whisk together the egg yolks and remaining sugar. Very slowly, start pouring the hot milk little by little into the egg mixture, whisking constantly. Pour the mixture back in the saucepan and cook over medium heat, stirring constantly, until the mixture coats the back of a spoon. Be careful not to boil. The sauce can be kept in the refrigerator until ready to use.

CINNAMON ROLLS WITH SWEET GLAZE

PREP TIME: 1 hour (plus 30 minutes for rising) | **COOK TIME:** 25–30 minutes | **SERVES:** 12 rolls

ROLLS

1 cup milk, room temperature

1 ½ tablespoons yeast

4 cups flour

6 tablespoons butter

½ cup sugar

2 eggs

Salt, pinch

FILLING

1 ½ cups brown sugar

1 tablespoon cinnamon

1 cup butter, room temperature

2 cups pecan pieces

1 cup sweetened condensed milk

GLAZE

½ cup brown sugar

6 tablespoons butter

2 ½ tablespoons sweetened condensed milk

2 tablespoons heavy cream

2 tablespoons sour cream

1 ½ teaspoons corn syrup

Salt, pinch

Vanilla extract, splash

½ teaspoon cinnamon

1. Grease 12 large muffin cups.
2. Lightly coat a large bowl with vegetable oil. Set aside.
3. Combine milk and yeast and let it sit until it bubbles. Combine flour, butter, and sugar in the bowl of a standing electric mixer fitted with the dough hook. Mix until just combined. Add the yeast mixture and start beating on medium speed for about 4 minutes, occasionally scraping down the sides of the bowl with a rubber spatula. The dough should be very smooth.
4. Transfer the dough to the coated bowl and cover with plastic wrap. Place in a draft-free spot to rise for 20 minutes or until volume is doubled. Once dough is ready, roll the dough out to a 9 x 24-inch rectangle on a lightly flowered work surface.
5. **TO MAKE FILLING:** In a small bowl, mix the brown sugar with the cinnamon. Spread the butter and sprinkle with the cinnamon, sugar, and pecans, and drizzle with sweetened condensed milk.
6. Beginning at a long edge, roll up the dough as tightly as possible and pinch the seam. Cut the log into twelve 2-inch pieces and set them in the muffin cups, cut-side up. Cover and let stand in a warm place for 30 minutes.
7. Preheat oven to 350 degrees. Set the muffin pan on a baking sheet and bake for 25–30 minutes, until the buns are golden brown.
8. **TO MAKE GLAZE:** In a small saucepan, bring the brown sugar, butter, sweetened condensed milk, heavy cream, sour cream, corn syrup, salt, vanilla, and cinnamon to a boil. Simmer until thickened slightly, about 3 minutes. Remove from the heat. Pour the glaze over the hot buns very slowly. Let stand until the buns have soaked up some of the glaze. Serve warm.

SPECIAL
OCCASIONS

Holidays and special occasions are the yearly markers on our revolving calendar that signal seasons, celebrations, and anticipated gatherings. Without them, the year would be a free fall with nothing to catch us, slow us down, or cause us to remember.

It would be like February all year. While my appreciation for food and its tie to community was nurtured at the family dinner table, the special gatherings also stand out in my mind. This is, of course, by design. For most of us the run-of-the-mill chicken and vegetable dinners we ate a thousand times as kids blur together even though these were the building blocks of our health and formation. But our memories pop with vivid color when it comes to the pastel chocolate eggs nestled in our Easter baskets. We can still taste the homemade peach ice cream we ate on the Fourth of July and the sweet potato casserole with the toasted marshmallows on Thanksgiving.

The foods we remember eating on special occasions stand out precisely because they were novel dishes, typically served on special days by special people. It was at these annual gatherings that I began to unwittingly associate certain family members with the dishes they were known for. My grandmother on my dad's side was the queen of the twice-baked potato, though in her later years and with her trademark sigh, she was big on letting us know how much trouble they had become—I think it was the *twice* part. She and my grandpa, who lived in Annapolis, Maryland, were also the purveyors of our seafood. Crab imperial, crab dip, and plump shrimp were regular attendees at our holiday celebrations. As a kid, I remember picking up on the fact that my parents and aunts and uncles had become increasingly concerned about the preparation of that seafood the further my grandparents crept into their eighties. "Meredith," my mom would ask my aunt by mid-afternoon, "how long has the shrimp been sitting out on the kitchen counter thawing?"

"Since 8:00 a.m.," my aunt would smile. "I'm working on it."

My grandparents were untouchable in my book, and if they left the seafood unrefrigerated for six hours, surely they knew something we didn't. Plus, we'd all been eating their dips for years and none of us had died yet. Despite the questionable practices, I had no idea how good I had it living in Northern Virginia, just an hour from their home by the Chesapeake Bay. It didn't occur to me that not everyone had blue crab in their grandparents' backyards.

To this day, as full-fledged adults, my siblings and I still expect our mom to make her famous Christmas recipes.

I learned at an early age that at Minter family gatherings, family members had important roles that couldn't be forsaken without significant backlash. It was incumbent upon my Aunt Carol Minter to bring her famous mashed potatoes (secret ingredient: horseradish). My Uncle Charlie oversaw the cooking of the tenderloin; it had to be the perfect state of rare, which was exactly one degree past still-mooing. (It was generally understood that if you preferred your meat well-done, you were somewhat of a lesser Minter.) My Uncle Jim had the lock on homemade eggnog at Christmastime. Aunt Meredith, from whom I take my middle name, selflessly concerned herself with what gap she could fill rather than what dish she wanted to make. You could always count on her for something classy. In addition to many other things, my mom made Rice Krispy desserts that looked like pinecones dusted with snow. My cousin Scotty claimed we couldn't truly have Christmas without them.

To this day, as full-fledged adults, my siblings and I still expect our mom to make her famous Christmas recipes. For the past several Decembers, my mom has sent an email to all the kids and in-laws, declaring that she cannot single handedly make each of us our favorite dishes, that she really needs us to pick up the slack, that she may not be able to make her Overnight Christmas French Toast because it's so much trouble. That email gets all of us adult kids totally bent out of shape (okay, maybe just two of us), and then every Christmas morning, out comes the Overnight French Toast, and later in the day the tenderloin, the special mashed potatoes, the crispy Brussels sprouts, and the latest desserts from the Style section of the *Washington Post*. Eventually, even the pinecones with "snow" show up. One day my mom will actually follow through on cutting back, and believe you me, it will be pandemonium.

This whole idea of special meals on special occasions is not so much about the dishes themselves as it is about the important principal of tradition. Maybe you've always stuffed your turkey with oyster stuffing like my friend April grew up doing. Or maybe you're like Mary Katharine and your mom made cornbread dressing that never touched the inside of the turkey's cavity. I've discovered firsthand that these established practices aren't easily parted with. April is from Detroit and Mary Katharine is from Rock Hill, South Carolina, all of which explain the Friendsgiving issues I begin mediating the day after Halloween. We've reached a settlement: we make both. The Thanksgiving sparring is because our allegiance to a certain dish is about more than food. It's about the family heritage and experiences that that food represents—how else can you possibly explain oyster stuffing?

You make a certain meal because it reminds you of how your grandmother used to do it. You use a certain carving knife because it's the one your dad used. You follow the tattered and oil-splattered recipe of a special relative in hopes of giving your children a taste of what you grew up enjoying. We pass on traditions to our kids and grandkids and nieces and nephews because we understand the significance of being tethered to lineage. Certain meals help us taste our heritage, reminding us of certain relatives, their personalities, and the values they stood for. Cooking and serving those meals to our own family and friends become a tangible display of what we, too, hope to be known for.

That God would pair cooking and food with these celebrations is something we should gladly take note of. When savory smells and flavorful tastes remind us of God's goodness in the presence of loved ones, we're keeping a feast that will one day be fully consummated in heaven.

In biblical terms the idea of gathering together at special times on special days can be traced all the way back to Exodus. The Israelites celebrated the Passover to commemorate their deliverance out of Egypt. They ate unleavened bread and sacrificed animals at the exact time in the evening that they were freed from Pharaoh's bondage. The foods they ate and the traditions they kept helped them remember God's faithfulness in their lives. Other types of biblical feasts celebrated God's covenant love, provision, and forgiveness. The fact that God would pair cooking and food with these celebrations is something we should gladly take note of. When savory smells and flavorful tastes remind us of God's goodness in the presence of loved ones, we're keeping a feast that will one day be fully consummated in heaven.

Until then our holiday gatherings will be a mix of utter bliss and also unmet longings, harried busyness, and maybe some misgivings over how the stuffing is being prepared. Or is it dressing? Given the craziness those kinds of gatherings often bring, I try to keep a few things in mind. First off, holidays aren't typically the time to try to fix your relatives. Take that task off your plate and make Regina's cheesecake instead. You may have legitimate grievances that need to be addressed, but I've found that in the kitchen ten minutes before the scalloped potatoes come out isn't the best time or place to deal with festering wounds. I also try to free myself from the cultural ideal of a perfect holiday. As a single woman, my Christmases and Thanksgivings will probably never resemble the commercials with kids bounding down the stairs in search of their stockings or a husband slicing up the tenderloin and then handing me the keys to a new Lexus that's sitting in the driveway with a bow on the hood. Then again, nobody's holidays look like that.

Holidays aren't typically the time to try to fix your relatives. Take that task off your plate and make Regina's cheesecake instead.

One way I combat unrealistic expectations that inevitably come with holidays and special occasions is to proactively set my attention and affection on Jesus. I try to let Him set the narrative. If I'm practicing thankfulness, looking for ways I can serve others, and contenting myself in Him while I go about my preparations, my experiences are generally filled with peace and joy. And when they're not, I'm honest with Him about the sensitive places on which these seasons tend to tug. Talking to Him while cooking is a balm to my soul. With these few loving pieces of advice in mind, here are some of Regina and my favorite holiday recipes that will make any special occasion memorable. Because this might be the year your mom decides to stop doing all the cooking. ❦

*Braised Lamb Shanks
with Polenta
(recipe on p. 206)*

Cabbage Au Gratin
(recipe on p. 207)

BRAISED LAMB SHANKS WITH POLENTA

LAMB SHANKS

PREP TIME: 20 minutes | **COOK TIME:** 5–6 hours | **SERVES:** 4

3 tablespoons olive oil

4 lamb shanks, trimmed

2 teaspoons salt

1 teaspoon fresh black pepper

2 medium onions, chopped

3 cloves garlic, minced

3 large carrots, chopped

1 ½ cups tomatoes, crushed

Optional: Substitute Canadian steak seasoning for salt and pepper

1. In a large skillet, heat olive oil over medium-high heat.
2. Rub the lamb with salt and pepper (or Canadian steak seasoning). Braise in skillet until browned on all sides. Remove from skillet. In the same skillet, add onions, garlic, and carrots, and stir occasionally until softened, about 5 minutes. Stir in tomatoes and then transfer to a Dutch oven. Then add the lamb shanks to the Dutch oven. Cover and cook on low heat until tender, about 5–6 hours.
3. Serve the shank on top of soft polenta and drizzle with sauce from Dutch oven.

POLENTA

PREP TIME: 15 minutes | **COOK TIME:** 25 minutes | **SERVES:** 4

3 cups boiling water

1 cup yellow cornmeal

1 cup heavy cream

2 tablespoons butter

¼ teaspoon sea salt

½ cup Parmesan cheese

1. Boil the water and slowly drop in the cornmeal, whisking constantly to not form lumps. Reduce heat to low, add the heavy cream and butter, and cook for 25 minutes.
2. Remove from heat. Add salt and Parmesan cheese.

Lamb shanks are a wonderful way to express that an occasion is important and help your guests feel special. It is easy to prepare and can be paired with many things as a side, but is best with polenta!

❖ Pictured on page 204

CABBAGE AU GRATIN

PREP TIME: 15 minutes | **COOK TIME:** 30–45 minutes | **SERVES:** 4–6

1 medium cabbage, quartered and cooked

Salt and peper, to taste

2 sticks butter, melted

1 cup Parmigiano Reggiano cheese, grated

2 cups plain bread crumbs

1. Preheat oven to 350 degrees. Note that this dish is assembled much like you would make lasagna.
2. Start by buttering a 9 x 13-inch baking dish. Layer the individual leaves of cabbage and top each layer with salt and pepper, a drizzle of butter, and a light coating of Parmigiano Reggiano cheese and bread crumbs. Repeat the layering until you reach the top of the dish, finishing it off with a top layer of cheese and bread crumbs.
3. Bake for about 30–45 minutes or until the top is a golden brown.

Cabbage may not be the most popular pick in the produce section of your local grocer, but this recipe might just make you a fan. Buttery, crisp, and cheesy—in my humble opinion, it's the best way to dress up any vegetable, especially cabbage!

Pictured on page 205 ❖

Brussels Sprouts
with Bacon
(recipe on p. 211)

Beef Stew
(recipe on p. 210)

208

Chessecake
(recipe on p. 212)

BEEF STEW

PREP TIME: 45 minutes | **COOK TIME:** 3 hours | **SERVES:** 4–6

2 tablespoons vegetable oil, divided

3–4 pounds boneless beef stew meat cut in cubes (can also use chuck roast or sirloin)

2 cups carrots, sliced

½ large onion, chopped

1 ½ cups pearl onions, peeled

2 cups tomatoes, unpeeled, cored, and chopped

1 teaspoon fresh thyme, chopped

3 cloves garlic, minced

1 tablespoon tomato paste

2 cups hot water

Salt and pepper, to taste

RUE

2 tablespoons butter

3 tablespoons flour

1. Add 1 tablespoon of vegetable oil in a frying pan over high heat. Add the meat to the pan, and brown as many pieces as will fit in one layer. Turn frequently to brown all sides. Transfer the beef to a casserole dish. Keep browning until all the meat is done.

2. Return the frying pan to the stove and add 1 tablespoon vegetable oil. Add the vegetables and let it simmer for 5 minutes until a little brown.

3. In a large braising casserole pan, add the meat, vegetables, tomatoes, thyme, garlic, tomato paste, and liquids. This liquid will be enough to cover the beef. Add more water if needed. Cook for 2–3 hours until very tender. Salt and pepper, to taste.

4. **TO MAKE RUE:** In a small saucepan melt the butter. Then add the flour and mix them well until a smooth paste is formed. Add 1/2 cup of the meat sauce and blend well. Keep adding more liquid to dissolve all the rue.

5. Add the rue to the meat and stir around to thicken the stew.

K

Whenever I eat dinner at Regina's house, I secretly hope she'll be making her beef stew. The cuts of meat she uses is important for its tenderness. You don't usually associate the phrase "melts in your mouth" with beef stew, but that's all I can think of when I eat this traditional meal.

❖ *Pictured on page 208*

BRUSSELS SPROUTS WITH BACON

PREP TIME: 10 minutes | **COOK TIME:** 15 minutes | **SERVES:** 4–6

3 pounds Brussels sprouts

½ cup bacon, chopped small

3 tablespoons butter

1 clove garlic, minced

Optional: Salt and pepper, to taste

1. Trim off the woody ends of the Brussels sprouts and cut them in half lengthwise.
2. In a skillet, fry the bacon pieces until crispy. Set aside.
3. Heat the butter in a saucepan large enough to hold all the Brussels sprouts. Add the garlic and cook on low heat about 2 minutes. Adjust the heat to medium and add the Brussels sprouts. Let them cook, turning them constantly to not burn. They should be tender but not too soft.
4. Add the bacon and serve hot.

Pictured on page 208 ❖

CHEESECAKE

PREP TIME: 20 minutes | **COOK TIME:** 1 hour 15 minutes | **SERVES:** 6–8

CRUST

2 cups vanilla (or chocolate) wafers, finely ground

¼ cup sugar

5 tablespoons butter, melted

CHEESECAKE

4 packages (8 ounces each) cream cheese

1 (14 ounce) can sweetened condensed milk

½ cup sugar

5 eggs

½ teaspoon vanilla

⅓ cup heavy cream

Salt, pinch

1. Preheat oven to 325 degrees. Butter a springform pan and cover with parchment paper (bottom and sides).
2. **FOR CRUST:** combine crust ingredients and press onto springform pan. Using your fingertips, bring the crust to the sides, covering about 1 inch up.
3. **FOR CHEESECAKE:** In a large bowl, using an electric mixer, beat together the cream cheese, sweetened condensed milk, and sugar until well-blended. Beat in the eggs one at the time until mixture is smooth. Then add vanilla, heavy cream, and salt until smooth. Pour the filling over the crust and cover with a foil wrap. Fill a baking pan with hot tap water to a depth of 1 inch and carefully place the cheesecake pan in it. Bake until the center barely shakes when the springform pan is shaken, about 50 minutes. Remove the cheesecake to a wire rack and let it cool. Refrigerate overnight.

CHOCOLATE CHEESECAKE

Follow the recipe instructions above, but once the cheesecake batter has been poured into the pan in step 3, add 1 cup melted dark chocolate. Swirl around to disperse and make a design. Continue recipe normally from there.

PEANUT BUTTER CHEESECAKE

Follow the recipe instructions above, but add 1 cup peanut butter to batter in step 3, and blend to disperse. Continue and follow recipe normally from there.

TALLER CHEESECAKES THAT INCLUDE CAKE LAYERS

If you desire the cheesecake to be taller, you can always bake the base as a cake layer, using a cake mix. For example, with chocolate cheesecake, I use one box of brownie cake mix, and bake according to the package. After the cake is baked, add the cheesecake batter and follow the instructions for baking the same as the cheesecake.

❖ *Pictured on page 209*

Party Pork Loin
(recipe on p. 216)

Charlotte's Pecan Pie
(recipe on p. 218)

Christmas Rice
(recipe on p. 217)

215

PARTY PORK LOIN

PREP TIME: 45 minutes | **COOK TIME:** 1 hour 30 minutes | **SERVES:** 6–8

FILLING

2 tablespoons butter

3 tablespoons brown sugar

5 apples, cut in cubes

1 teaspoon lemon juice

PORK LOIN

1 pork loin, boneless
(4 pounds)

1 ½ teaspoon salt
(more if needed)

1 ½ teaspoons black pepper
(more if needed)

2 cloves garlic, crushed
(more if needed)

1 tablespoon onion powder

1. **TO PREPARE FILLING:** Melt the butter in a skillet. Then add the brown sugar, apples, and lemon juice. Cook for about 5 minutes. Set aside.

2. **TO PREPARE PORK LOIN:** Preheat oven to 375 degrees. Butterfly the pork loin by making a lengthwise cut down center of flat side, cutting to within 1/2 inch of other side. Do not cut all the way through pork. Open pork, forming a rectangle. Flatten to 1-inch thick using a meat mallet or rolling pin. Sprinkle the meat with salt, pepper, garlic, and onion powder.

3. Spoon the apple mixture over pork and roll up, jelly roll fashion. Tie with string at 1 1/2-inch intervals. Sprinkle with remaining salt, pepper, garlic, and onion.

4. Roast in the oven until the meat is done, about 30–45 minutes.

CHRISTMAS RICE

PREP TIME: 30 minutes | **COOK TIME:** 54 minutes | **SERVES:** 6–8

4 tablespoons butter

20 pearl onions

1 ½ cups wild rice

5 ½ cups chicken broth

1 ½ cups long grain rice

1 cup dried apricots, coarsely chopped

1 cup raisins

¾ cup dried cranberries

2 tablespoons fresh thyme, chopped

1 ½ cups pecans, toasted and chopped

Salt and pepper, to taste

1. Melt 2 tablespoons butter in a large skillet over medium heat. Add pearl onions and sauté until light brown. Set aside.

2. In a large saucepan, melt 2 tablespoons butter. Add wild rice and stir to coat all the rice with the butter. Add chicken broth. Bring to a boil, reduce heat to low, cover, and simmer for 30 minutes.
   Add the long grain rice and continue to simmer until the rices are tender and liquid is almost absorbed, about 20 minutes.

3. Stir in the apricots, raisins, cranberries, and thyme. Cover and simmer for 4 minutes longer. Stir in the pearl onions and the rest of the butter. Mix in pecans. Season with salt and pepper, to taste.

Pictured on page 215 ❖

CHARLOTTE'S PECAN PIE

PREP TIME: 10 minutes | **COOK TIME:** 1 hour 15–20 minutes | **SERVES:** 6–8

1 cup sugar

¾ cup light Karo syrup

3 eggs

½ stick butter, melted

1 teaspoon, vanilla

1 cup pecan pieces

1 unbaked deep-dish pie shell

1. Preheat oven to 325 degrees.
2. Mix all ingredients together in a mixing bowl and pour into pie shell.
3. Bake for 1 hour 15–20 minutes, then reduce heat to 300 degrees and bake until brown and set.

❖ *Pictured on page 215*

Chicken Spinach with
Puff Pastry
(recipe on p. 222)

*Mom's Romaine Salad
(recipe on p. 224)*

*Asparagus with
Pine Nuts and Parmesan
(recipe on p. 223)*

CHICKEN SPINACH WITH PUFF PASTRY

PREP TIME: 45 minutes | **COOK TIME:** 20–25 minutes | **SERVES:** 6–8

1 rotisserie chicken, deboned and shredded

2 packages (10 ounces each) frozen spinach, thawed and drained

½ teaspoon garlic powder

½ teaspoon onion powder

Salt and pepper, to taste

1 (12 ounce) package cream cheese

2 cups Cheddar cheese, room temperature

2 puff pastry sheets (Pepperidge Farm)

2 egg yolks, for brushing

Optional: Poppy seeds or sesame seeds

1. Preheat oven to 350 degrees. Line a baking sheet with parchment paper.
2. In a large bowl, mix together the shredded chicken, spinach, spices, and cheeses.
3. On a lightly floured surface, roll out each puff pastry sheet into a rectangle, approximately 11 x 13 inches. Divide the chicken and spinach mixture between the two sheets and layer each half. Brush the edges of the puff pastry sheets with egg yolks.
4. Roll so the filling is fully enclosed. Fold the ends and put on the baking sheet lined with parchment paper, seam-side down. Brush the top of each with egg yolk.
5. Here's where you can be creative. Cut out shapes from the excess puff pastry and place them on top of the roll, brushing with the egg yolk to ensure they stick.
6. Bake for 20–25 minutes or until golden brown.

Ⓡ | *This is a creamy and comforting take on chicken, which lends itself to being as fancy a dish or as simple as you'd like. Feel free to sprinkle the rolls with poppy seeds or sesame seeds if you're feeling creative!*

❖ *Pictured on page 220*

ASPARAGUS WITH PINE NUTS AND PARMESAN

PREP TIME: 15 minutes | **COOK TIME:** 15 minutes | **SERVES:** 6–8

1 cup pine nuts, toasted

2 pounds asparagus

Salt and pepper, to taste

4 tablespoons butter

Parmesan cheese, large shaved pieces

Lemon cut into wedges for serving

1. Preheat an oven to 300 degrees. Toast the pine nuts on a baking sheet in oven (or use a frying pan, stirring constantly) until lightly colored and fragrant. Set aside.

2. Cut off any tough, white, or woody ends of the asparagus and discard. To make your asparagus al dente, put them on a microwave-safe platter and microwave on high for 5 minutes (more if needed), depending on your likes. Add salt and pepper, to taste.

3. Brown butter in skillet and pour over asparagus, add the pine nuts and shavings of Parmesan cheese. Serve with lemon wedges.

Pictured on page 221 ❖

MOM'S ROMAINE SALAD

PREP TIME: 15 minutes | **COOK TIME:** 5 minutes | **SERVES:** 6–8

SALAD INGREDIENTS

10 cups romaine lettuce,
   torn into small pieces

Vegetable oil

1 cup pecan halves

3 tablespoons maple syrup

VINAIGRETTE

1 clove garlic, finely chopped

1 tablespoon shallots,
   finely chopped

¼ teaspoon salt

¼ teaspoon pepper,
   freshly ground

2 tablespoons maple syrup

2 teaspoons Dijon mustard

2 tablespoons red wine vinegar

6 tablespoons vegetable oil

1. Preheat oven to 375 degrees. Lightly oil 2 baking sheets with vegetable oil. Tear romaine lettuce and place in large salad bowl.
2. **FOR PECAN TOPPING:** In small bowl, combine the pecans and maple syrup and toss gently to combine. Spread pecans in single layer on one of the sheets. Roast in preheated oven, stirring once, until syrup is bubbling, about 5 minutes. Immediately scrape the pecans onto the other prepared sheet, spreading them out to cool.
3. **FOR VINAIGRETTE:** In small bowl, whisk together the garlic, shallots, salt, pepper, maple syrup, Dijon mustard, and red wine vinegar. Whisking constantly, slowly add the vegetable oil in steady stream.
4. **TO ASSEMBLE SALAD:** Drizzle salad with vinaigrette dressing, and sprinkle roasted pecans on top. Serve immediately.

K

My mom is such a good cook but she's one of those people who doesn't write anything down. She just does a little bit of this and a little of that, and you never know quite how. I begged her to put this down on paper so I could pass it along to you. The dressing is worth the price of this recipe.

❖ *Pictured on page 221*

TWICE-BAKED POTATO

PREP TIME: 30 minutes | **COOK TIME:** 15–18 minutes | **SERVES:** 4–6

4 large baking potatoes

4 tablespoons butter

½ cup heavy cream

1 teaspoon chives

1 cup Cheddar cheese

½ cup sour cream

Salt and pepper, to taste

6 slices bacon, fried and broken into small pieces

1. Bake the potatoes in oven or microwave until done. If using oven, bake at 350 degrees until soft. If using microwave, about 7 minutes for each potato. Allow to cool.

2. Preheat oven to 400 degrees.

3. Keeping the skins intact, carefully slice 1 inch of skin off the top and scoop out the pulp. Place the pulp in a bowl.

4. Mash the potatoes and mix in the butter, heavy cream, chives, Cheddar cheese, sour cream, salt, and pepper. Spoon the mixture back into the potato shells, piling high. Sprinkle with bacon pieces and bake for 15 minutes. Remove from oven, sprinkle with chives, and serve hot.

SEASONAL DRINKS

Seasonal drinks add a nice touch to your entertaining, but don't add too much to your budget or preparation capacity. In the summertime, I love mixing sparkling water with cranberry juice. It's refreshing, colorful, and you can dress it up with a slice of lime on the rim. My niece and nephew love it and regularly ask if I can make them what they fondly refer to as their "special spicy drink." Instead of cranberry juice you can also use a tablespoon of cherry concentrate. Cherries are high in antioxidants and the flavor is one of my favorites.

Another simple year-round option is water infused with seasonal fruits and herbs, contained in a quality glass vase or dispenser. Citrus, melons, berries, ginger, and herbs like basil, mint, and rosemary can be mixed and matched for flavorful and healthy drinks. The cut fruits and herbs also offer a visually pleasing presentation.

> Another simple year-round option is water infused with seasonal fruits and herbs, contained in a quality glass vase or dispenser.

In the fall I never tire of hot cider simmering on the stove with cinnamon sticks and cloves. Recipes abound online, and any version will fill every crevice of your home with an inviting aroma, warming the hearts of your friends and family. I also try to keep an assortment of teas on hand and a quality jar of local honey. English black tea with a splash of milk, or a fine green tea with a hint of honey are some of my favorites. Never am I without a good bag of coffee beans, cream, and sugar for anyone who thrives on caffeine.

One of my oldest and fondest memories, especially over Christmas, is of my dad making us homemade hot chocolate. He wouldn't dare compromise with the instant-powder versions. "Let me show you kids how this is done," he'd say, leaning over the stovetop. For a single cup he'd dump a heaping teaspoon of unsweetened cocoa, a tablespoon of sugar, and a dash of salt into a small saucepan. After adding just enough water to make a paste, he'd heat the cocoa over medium-high heat, add 1/8 cup of half-and-half and a cup of milk (no one said this was healthy), and stir until heated. A few marshmallows on top, and we were the happiest kids in the neighborhood. I love making his version of hot cocoa to this day.

If you're looking for something healthier, I've been enjoying a ginger, lime, and honey concoction that's great for your gut and also good for fighting off viruses. I cut off an inch or two of ginger, peel it, and cut it into thin slices. I boil the ginger in a few cups of water, depending on how strong you like it, then simmer covered for twenty minutes. After straining the ginger, I add a squeeze of fresh lime juice and a teaspoon of honey. Stir and enjoy. (You can boil the ginger one to two more times after the initial use.)

Whatever the season or occasion, don't forget about the drinks. Whether you're dressing up something as basic to our survival as water, arranging a few cold beverages in an inexpensive silver or copper drink tub, or simmering something warm on the stove during the colder months, your friends and family will feel welcomed into your home at the first sip. ❖

SWEET
CELEBRATIONS

Celebrations are good for the soul. Whether celebrating people, landmark events, or God's faithfulness, it's healthy to throw a party every now and again. Celebrations remind us that, in the midst of the monotony and sometimes hardships of life, there is still laughter, fellowship, and dancing to be found—birthdays, weddings, graduations, baptisms, baby showers, retirement parties.

They summon our attention and excitement, causing us to pause and rejoice. They give us an excuse to tear open sacks of sugar, unwrap sticks of butter, crack open eggs and not worry about the plumes of flour settling on every surface of the kitchen. They give us reason to bake with rich ingredients and not feel bad about it—let's be honest; you simply cannot celebrate with celery. And as we eat the Cherry-Almond Tart or Four Leches Cake, we don't ever have to mention how many calories are in each bite and how we're going to do better tomorrow. This is all implied information. From now on let's just assume that *we're all going to start eating healthy in the morning.*

One of the many reasons I loved working with Regina on this cookbook is that she's a professional baker and chocolatier who specializes in creating desserts from scratch.

Rule #39 from Michael Pollan's book *Food Rules* is "Eat all the junk food you want as long as you cook it yourself." His point is that homemade desserts, with real as opposed to synthetic ingredients, take time to create. If you only eat the treats you're willing to put the time into

making, you'll eat less of them—or at least that's the idea. One of the many reasons I loved working with Regina on this cookbook is that she's a professional baker and chocolatier who specializes in creating desserts from scratch. You won't make these desserts every day, but you won't need to. You'll pull them out for the celebrations that call for them. (Or just because you want them on a Tuesday night after work, and that's fine too.)

I wonder what celebrations stand out in your memory—what made them special and who was being celebrated, what foods were served and if there were any elements of surprise. A couple summers ago I was in the Eastern European country of Moldova and happened upon a celebration I'd not expected. Moldova is a reserved culture, somewhat stoic in nature. When you think, *let's party*, it's not the first place that comes to mind, which I'm pretty sure is all part of their ruse.

I was there celebrating the graduation of thirteen girls and eleven boys from Justice & Mercy International's Transitional Living Program. It's a three-year program for some of the country's most vulnerable children, many who have spent their childhoods in orphanages. I sat and watched each of these beautiful, courageous teenagers receive their diplomas in their caps and gowns. The gravity of what these kids had come from and the opportunities that lay ahead was cause for reflection and sobriety. And then the band started playing.

Before I knew it, the band was in full swing, cake was making the rounds, and every houseparent and child had broken out into a traditional Moldovan folk dance under the night's sky.

Never underestimate the vigor or stamina of Moldovan musicians playing the hammered dulcimer, violin, pan flute, accordion, and bagpipes. Before I knew it, the band was in full swing, cake was making the rounds, and every houseparent and child had broken out into a traditional Moldovan folk dance under the night's sky. They were synchronized, limber, and clapping. Their ability to go from prim and proper to a singing dance troupe in a New York minute is their great national secret. And so it occurred to me why Moldovans are so reserved—they're storing all their energy up for the dancing!

Someone grabbed my hand, and without me realizing what had happened, I was swept into the circle, briskly flying around the courtyard, singing Romanian words and trying to get my appendages to cooperate with Moldovan protocol. Petru, one of the new graduates, took my hand and asked me to be his partner. I went bug-eyed. These were terrifying words, but this night was not about me and my awkwardness, but about the kids from our program: Petru, Zita, Costa, Tanea, Maria, Ala, and Tudor. So off Petru and I went to the beat of the accordion. I noticed that the really good partners were taking turns moving to the center of the dance floor while the surrounding circle hooted and hollered. I was gaining confidence. "Petru!" I yelled over the pan flute, "Let's move to the center!" I'll never forget the horror on his face. "No, Kelly!" he said in his thick Moldovan accent, "We are not middle material!" He had a point, but if having the most fun makes you a good Moldovan folk dancer, we would have won the night.

> ## For the father, a celebration was not optional. His son had returned and a feast with music and dancing was the only reasonable response.

At some point while being swung around that circle under the glow of the moon I had the distinct thought that this was the most fun I'd had in years. Up to that point in my life, I only *thought* I knew what it meant to celebrate. I was on the other side of the world without the cares of everyday life, without my normal inhibitions such as *I can't dance*, celebrating redemption. Celebrating these kids who had been delivered out of horrific environments and brought into loving homes, now ready to take on the world. Celebrating our cross-cultural friendships and our deep fellowship through the person of Jesus. After all these kids had been through and all they'd accomplished, we simply had to celebrate. No other response would have been adequate.

In Luke 15, Jesus tells a story about a father who celebrated the return of his younger son. It reminds me not only of the opportunity, but also the responsibility we have to celebrate. When the younger son arrived home after squandering his inheritance on partying and prostitutes, his father was surprisingly filled with compassion. Seeing his son in the distance, he gathered his robe and ran through the fields unencumbered, throwing his arms around him. He said to his servants, " 'Bring the fattened calf and slaughter it, and let's celebrate with a feast, because this son of mine was dead and is alive again; he was lost and is found!' So they began to celebrate" (Luke 15:23–24). *A feast*. The richest foods, the fattest calf, Regina's strawberry cake (my rendition) were the centerpiece of the celebration. We can't miss the part that food plays in the story.

The father explained to the older brother, your wayward brother was lost and now is found, he was dead and is now alive, "We *had* to celebrate" (Luke 15:32, emphasis mine).

For the father, a celebration was not optional. His son had returned and a feast with music and dancing was the only reasonable response. For the children in Moldova who'd come through unspeakable hardship, their graduation necessitated a fete of epic proportions. I don't know what special people or milestones you'll be celebrating this year, but if you can't hire a Moldovan band, a well-crafted dessert made with unfettered joy will go a long way. Make something from scratch. Pull out all the stops. The gift of life and the goodness of God are not only our delight to celebrate, but also our responsibility. Sometimes celebration is simply incumbent upon us. It's not just that we could or should or might cook something wonderful, but that we simply *have* to. ❧

* Michael Pollan, *Food Rules: An Eater's Manual* (New York: Penguin Books, 2009).

BIRTHDAY STRAWBERRY CAKE

PREP TIME: 1 hour 15 minutes (plus 2 hours refrigeration) | **COOK TIME:** 50 minutes | **SERVES:** 12–16

FILLING

1 ½ pounds fresh strawberries, sliced (reserve 5 whole for decoration)

3 tablespoons sugar

1 (14 ounce) can sweetened condensed milk

2 cans milk (use sweetened condensed milk can for measurements)

4 egg yolks

¾ teaspoon vanilla

2 tablespoons corn starch

1 (8 ounce) can table cream

WHIPPED CREAM

4 cups heavy cream

2 tablespoons sugar

CAKE

1 tablespoon butter, softened

6 eggs, separated

3 cups sugar

10 tablespoons hot milk

3 cups flour

1 ½ teaspoons baking powder

1. **FOR THE STRAWBERRIES:** In a small bowl, combine the sliced strawberries (reserve 5 for decoration) with 3 tablespoons of sugar and stir. Cover with plastic wrap and let the bowl sit in the refrigerator for about 2 hours, until the strawberries begin to release their juices.

2. **FOR THE FILLING:** In a medium saucepan, over medium heat, whisk together sweetened condensed milk, milk, egg yolks, vanilla, and corn starch. Cook, whisking constantly, until cream thickens into a pastry-cream consistency. Pour the cream into a bowl and add the table cream. Mix well. Then cover with plastic wrap, pressing it directly onto the surface of the cream to avoid forming a skin. Place in the refrigerator to cool.

3. **FOR THE WHIPPED CREAM:** In a large bowl, beat the heavy whipping cream together with sugar until soft peaks form. Refrigerate until ready to use.

4. **FOR THE CAKE:** Use 1 tablespoon butter to grease a 12-inch round cake pan and line with parchment paper. Preheat the oven to 350 degrees.

5. In a small bowl, beat the egg whites with a hand mixer until soft peaks form.

6. In the bowl of an electric mixer, beat the egg yolks and sugar until pale and fluffy. Add milk slowly, beating constantly. Turn the mixer to low speed and add flour and baking powder until well-combined. Gently fold in the egg whites with the help of a spatula.

7. Pour the batter into the pan and bake for about 20–25 minutes, until a toothpick inserted in the center of the cake comes out clean. Let cool and turn the cake out onto a platter. Using a long serrated knife, gently divide the cake into 3 layers.

8. **TO ASSEMBLE THE FINISHED CAKE:** Start by generously brushing the bottom layer of cake with the juices from the strawberries. Layer on half the sliced strawberries, then 1/3 cup of the filling, then 2/3 cup of the whipped cream. Repeat the layering over the second round of cake, not forgetting to brush the round with strawberry juice. Add the top layer, brush with juice, and allow the cake to rest in the refrigerator for a hour. Cover the cake in whipped cream and decorate the top with the 5 whole strawberries. Voila! Our favorite birthday cake!

Four Leches Cake
(recipe on p. 240)

Mocha Torte
(recipe on p. 241)

FOUR LECHES CAKE

PREP TIME: 20 minutes (plus 3 hours refrigeration) | **COOK TIME:** 25 minutes | **SERVES:** 6–8

CAKE

Butter

1 ½ cups flour

Salt, pinch

1 tablespoon baking powder

3 eggs

1 cup sugar

1 teaspoon vanilla extract

½ cup whole milk

TOPPING

1 (14 ounce) can coconut milk

1 ¼ cups heavy cream

1 (14 ounce) can evaporated milk

1 (14 ounce) can sweetened condensed milk

Ground cinnamon, pinch

Ground cloves, pinch

1. Preheat oven to 350 degrees.
2. Butter a 9 x 13-inch glass baking dish.
3. In a large bowl, mix together the flour, salt, and baking powder. Set aside.
4. In the bowl of an electric mixer, beat the eggs, sugar, and vanilla extract until light and fluffy. Add half of the flour mixture at a low speed until just blended. Slowly add the milk and the rest of the flour mixture.
5. Pour the batter into the baking dish and bake for about 25 minutes. Remove from oven and let rest.
6. **TO PREPARE THE TOPPING:** In a saucepan, mix the coconut milk, heavy cream, evaporated milk, sweetened condensed milk, cinnamon, and cloves. Let boil over medium heat for 3 minutes. Remove from heat and let stand for 15 minutes.
7. Poke holes into the cake using a fork, and gradually pour the milk mixture over the entire cake. Cover the cake and refrigerate for about 3 hours.

❖ *Pictured on page 238*

MOCHA TORTE

PREP TIME: 10 minutes | **COOK TIME:** 35 minutes | **SERVES:** 6–8

7 ounces dark chocolate (61% cacao)

2 tablespoons instant coffee granules

¾ cup butter

5 eggs, separated

1 cup sugar

½ cup flour

1 teaspoon baking powder

1. Preheat oven to 350 degrees.
2. Line the base of a 9-inch pan with parchment paper.
3. Place dark chocolate, instant coffee granules, and butter in a bowl and set it over a pan with simmering water to melt.
4. Whisk the egg yolks with sugar until mixture turns pale. Fold in the flour and baking powder. Then add melted chocolate mixture, stirring gently.
5. In the bowl of an electric mixer, beat the egg whites until stiff and fold gently into the chocolate mixture. Transfer to the pan and bake for about 35 minutes. (The cake should be gooey in the center.) Cool completely before removing from the pan. The cake will sink in the middle.
6. For a more decadent finishing, you can always top the cake with chocolate ganache.

Pictured on page 239 ❖

Milk Chocolate,
White Chocolate, and
Toffee Chip Cookies
(recipe on p. 244)

Raspberry Linzer Cookies
(recipe on p. 245)

Pecan and Orange Cookies
(recipe on p. 246)

*Old-School Peanut
Butter Brownies
(recipe on p. 247)*

243

MILK CHOCOLATE, WHITE CHOCOLATE, AND TOFFEE CHIP COOKIES

PREP TIME: 20 minutes | **COOK TIME:** 8–10 minutes | **SERVES:** 60 cookies

2 cups butter, softened

2 cups sugar

2 cups brown sugar, packed

4 large eggs

2 teaspoons vanilla

5 cups quick oats

4 cups flour

1 teaspoon salt

2 teaspoons baking soda

2 teaspoons baking powder

2 cups white chocolate chip

2 cups semi-sweet chocolate chip

½ cup toffee bits

Cooking spray

1. Preheat oven to 350 degrees.
2. In a large bowl, mix butter, sugar, and brown sugar with a mixer at medium speed until light and fluffy. Add eggs and vanilla, stirring until just blended.
3. In a food processor, pulse oats until they reach the consistency of a fine powder.
4. In a separate bowl, combine powdered oats, flour, salt, baking soda, and baking powder. Stir until blended. Add dry mixture to the butter mixture 1 cup at a time, beating after every addition until blended. Stir in the chocolate chips and toffee bits.
5. Create 1-inch balls from the dough, and place 2 inches apart on a lightly greased cookie sheet.
6. Bake for 8–10 minutes or until browned. Remove and let sit for 3 minutes. Then, remove from the cookie sheet and cool completely on wire racks.

❖ *Pictured on page 242*

RASPBERRY LINZER COOKIES

PREP TIME: 20 minutes (plus 2 hours for refrigeration) | **COOK TIME:** 14 minutes | **SERVES:** 20 cookies

2 cups butter,
    room temperature

1 ½ cups sugar

½ teaspoon vanilla paste

2 ½ cups almonds, ground

3 eggs

5 cups flour

1 teaspoon cinnamon

Salt, pinch

Raspberry jam for filling

1. In a large bowl, beat butter, sugar, and vanilla paste until creamy. Then beat in ground almonds. Add eggs, one at a time, beating well after each addition.

2. In a large bowl, mix the flour and cinnamon. Then add butter mixture, beating just until combined. Divide dough into 2 rounds. Cover each with plastic wrap and refrigerate for 2 hours.

3. Preheat oven to 325 degrees and line a baking sheet with parchment paper. Roll half of the dough on lightly floured surface to 1/4-inch thickness. Using a round cookie cutter, cut 2 1/2-inch round cookies. Then, using a small heart cookie cutter, cut the heart in the center of each cookie.

4. Roll the other half of the dough to 1/4-inch thick, and cut 2 1/2-inch round cookies.

5. Place cookies 1 inch apart on cookie sheet and bake until edges are lightly brown, around 14 minutes. Let them cool on pans.

6. Spread 1 teaspoon of jam on each round cookie. Then cover with the cut-out heart cookies.

NOTE: Depending on the season, you can cut different shapes for these cookies—Christmas tree, star, bunny, clover—get creative!

I don't think I'll ever stop loving chocolate desserts, but I've also grown to appreciate the subtler, less sweet desserts like shortbread with a cup of tea. Maybe it's my trips to England that did this to me. Not only are these great for an afternoon treat, they're beautiful to display at a gathering.

Pictured on page 242 ❖

PECAN AND ORANGE COOKIES

PREP TIME: 15 minutes | **COOK TIME:** 12–16 minutes | **SERVES:** 20

17 tablespoons butter, unsalted, room temperature

¾ cup confectioner's powdered sugar

1 cup pecans, finely chopped

1 ½ teaspoons orange zest (2 tablespoons candied orange peel, cut very thin, can be substituted here)

2 ½ cups flour

Whole pecans, enough for cookie topping

Crystal sugar, for sprinkles

1. Preheat oven to 350 degrees. Line a cookie sheet (or two) with parchment paper.

2. In the bowl of an electric mixer, combine butter and confectioner's powdered sugar until creamy and pale yellow. Add pecans, orange zest, and flour, and mix until well-combined.

3. With a cookie scooper, create small balls from the dough and place them on a cookie sheet lined with parchment paper. Flatten the cookies lightly.

4. To decorate, use half of a pecan on top of each cookie and dust with crystal sugar. Then bake for about 12–16 minutes.

❖ *Pictured on page 242*

OLD-SCHOOL PEANUT BUTTER BROWNIES

PREP TIME: 15 minutes | **COOK TIME:** 25–30 minutes | **SERVES:** 6

BROWNIE

2 cups flour

2 teaspoons baking powder

⅔ cup butter

1 cup peanut butter

1 cup sugar

1 cup brown sugar

4 eggs

1 teaspoon vanilla

ICING

1 stick butter

6 tablespoons milk

4 tablespoons cocoa

1 (16 ounce) bag confectioner's powdered sugar

1. Preheat oven to 350 degrees and grease a 9 x 13-inch pan. Mix flour and baking powder together in a medium bowl and set aside.

2. In a large bowl, beat butter, peanut butter, and sugars together. Add eggs one at a time, and then add vanilla. Once mixed, fold dry ingredients into wet.

3. Spread the mixture into the greased pan. Bake for 25–30 minutes. Brownies are done when they just begin to pull away from the sides of the pan and are set in the center. Let brownies cool while you make the chocolate icing.

4. **FOR ICING:** Melt butter in saucepan with milk and cocoa. Stir. When bubbly, take off the heat and add a bag of confectioner's powdered sugar. Whisk until smooth. Spread on cooled brownies and serve.

Pictured on page 243 ❖

BANOFFI PIE

PREP TIME: 10 minutes | **COOK TIME:** 50 minutes | **SERVES:** 6–8

1 ½ cups graham cracker crumbs

10 tablespoons butter, melted

2 cans (14 ounces each) sweetened condensed milk (becomes caramel)

1 ½ cups heavy whipping cream

⅓ cup confectioner's powdered sugar

1 teaspoon vanilla

½ teaspoon instant coffee (powdered)

3 large bananas, sliced

Freshly ground coffee or chocolate shavings

1. Preheat oven to 350 degrees.

2. Mix graham cracker crumbs with melted butter. Then press into a 9-inch pie plate. Bake for 5–8 minutes. Allow to cool.

3. Immerse the unopened cans of sweetened condensed milk in a deep pan of boiling water. Cover and boil for 3 hours, making sure the cans remain covered with water. (Add water as needed.) Remove the cans from the water; allow to cool completely before opening. Once opened, it will have transformed into caramel.

4. Whip the cream with powdered sugar, vanilla, and instant coffee until thick and smooth.

5. On top of the crust, spread 1/3 of the caramel. Then add a layer of bananas. Repeat this layering two more times. Finally, spoon or pipe on the cream and lightly sprinkle with the freshly ground coffee or chocolate shavings.

I ate this at the Hungry Monk Restaurant in England where it was invented!

MEME'S POUND CAKE

PREP TIME: 15 minutes (plus 1 hour refrigeration) | **COOK TIME:** 1 hour | **SERVES:** 8–10

BERRY MIXTURE

2 cups strawberries, stems removed and sliced

2 cups blueberries

2 cups raspberries

¾ cup sugar

POUND CAKE

2 cups butter

3 cups sugar

6 eggs

3 cups flour

1 cup milk

1 tablespoon lemon zest

1 teaspoon vanilla

1 ½ teaspoons baking powder

1. Preheat oven to 350 degrees. Butter a Bundt cake pan and sprinkle with flour.
2. Combine all ingredients for berry mixture and let stand for at least 1 hour in refrigerator to macerate.
3. In the bowl of an electric mixer, beat butter and sugar until pale and fluffy. Add the eggs one at the time, mixing well. Add the flour and milk in alternating turns. Then add lemon zest, vanilla, and baking powder. Pour the batter into the Bundt pan and bake for about 1 hour until a toothpick placed in the center of the cake comes out clean.
4. Slice pound cake and serve with berry mixture on top.

Instead of berries, feel free to use whatever fresh fruits are in season. Peaches and nectarines make a wonderful topping as well. To enhance this dessert even more, add whipped cream!

CHERRY-ALMOND TART

PREP TIME: 45 minutes | **COOK TIME:** 45 minutes–1 hour (plus 10 minutes for chilling) | **SERVES:** 6–8

TART PASTRY

1 ¾ cups flour

Salt, pinch

½ cup sugar

3 egg yolks

1 teaspoon vanilla

CHERRY-ALMOND FILLING

8 tablespoons butter, softened

½ cup sugar

1 egg

1 egg yolk

¾ cup almonds, ground

Salt, pinch

2 cups cherries, pitted

Confectioner's powdered sugar for dusting

Whipped cream for serving

1. **TO MAKE TART PASTRY:** Mix the flour, salt, sugar, egg yolks, and vanilla. Work with your fingers until coarse crumbs form. Knead the dough until smooth and pliable. Shape the dough into a ball, cover with plastic wrap, and refrigerate for 30 minutes.

2. **TO MAKE CHERRY-ALMOND FILLING:** Use an electric mixer to blend butter and sugar until soft and pale yellow in color. Gradually add the egg and egg yolk. Then add the ground almonds and salt. Do not over mix.

3. Preheat oven to 350 degrees. Take dough out of refrigerator and roll out, laying it over a 9-inch tart tin. Add the almond filling as a layer on top of the dough. Then arrange the cherries, stem-end down, in concentric circles on top of the filling. Chill the tart in refrigerator for 10 minutes. Then bake for about 40–45 minutes until pastry starts to pull from the sides of the tin.

4. To serve, dust with confectioner's powdered sugar and add a dollop of whipped cream on each slice.

Try this one during cherry season. Pitting them might be a bit tedious but the effort is well worth it. I love this recipe because it's not overly sugary, and the cherries and almonds come together for a sweet and nutty flavor.

K

SHOPPING AND DINNER PARTY PREPARATION

(Kelly) I tend to be last-minute when it comes to preparations for a dinner party. If I make it to the grocery store a full day ahead of time, I feel like such an adult that the surrounding peace and organization is almost unsettling. I'm usually dashing around like a madwoman, sticking my neck across the finish line,

---

She's taught me that a peaceful presentation isn't a code that only domestic powerhouses can crack.

---

having either no makeup on or no toilet paper in the guest bathroom. This is why being around Regina has been so good for me. She's taught me that a peaceful presentation isn't a code that only domestic powerhouses can crack. All it takes is a little planning and preparation. Who knew?

(Regina) Growing up my mother and grandmother were always cooking, and it felt like everything we did revolved around the kitchen. I can still smell and taste the delicious dishes they would create from a simple wood-burning stove that was the heart of our home in Brazil. I was always in awe of how easy they made it look and how much love and pride they poured into serving others. Following in their footsteps, I've discovered the same happiness in watching people enjoy my food. Bringing friends and family together for a party is not as difficult as you might think. Here are a few great lessons I've learned through the years:

1. **Prepare your menu a few days ahead so that there's time to make changes.** Remember to choose a couple of dishes you can make ahead of the party, like desserts or sides, so that on the big day you'll have plenty of time to cook and still enjoy your guests.

2. **Make a list.** I try to make a shopping list at least two days before the party to make sure I don't forget anything.

3. **Read the recipes from beginning to end before you start to cook** and make sure you have all the ingredients you'll need. One day before the party I like to separate my ingredients into different trays with a copy of the recipe on top. It makes it so much easier to get straight to work when the time comes.

4. **A beautifully set table goes a long way.** If you love to garden, fresh flowers bring a special

Bringing friends and family together for a party is not as difficult as you might think.

oven on low heat. I make sure that my kitchen is completely clean before guests arrive so that only the smell of food draws them in. As the party begins, I'll start plating appetizers and serving drinks, and then it's time to simply enjoy!

(Kelly) I try to remember that a clean house, aptly set table, and having my grocery shopping completed ahead of time aren't ends in themselves. Instead, they aid in serving the people who are coming over. When I can prepare ahead of time, I find that instead of giving my focus to the pressing to-dos milling around my mind, I can give that attention to the faces and stories that are milling around my home. I have more capacity to focus on *people*—and isn't that the point? Why, yes, cooking and entertaining are forever and always about the people. ❖

touch, and remember that bigger isn't always better. Small vases with a few well-placed flowers and stems can be just as lovely. If you're entertaining at night, candles bring warmth to a space. Place a few around the kitchen as well to carry that feeling all the way through your home.

5. Remember to have fun when you cook! Play your favorite music and relax (easier said than done, I know, but always worth a try). Follow the recipes and keep everything warm in a warming drawer or in the

UNIVERSAL CONVERSION CHART

OVEN TEMPERATURE EQUIVALENTS

250°F = 120°C   400°F = 200°C
275°F = 135°C   425°F = 220°C
300°F = 150°C   450°F = 230°C
325°F = 160°C   475°F = 240°C
350°F = 180°C   500°F = 260°C
375°F = 190°C

MEASUREMENT EQUIVALENTS

Measurements should always be level unless directed otherwise.

1/8 teaspoon = 0.5 mL

1/4 teaspoon = 1 mL

1/2 teaspoon = 2 mL

1 teaspoon = 5 mL

1 tablespoon = 3 teaspoons = 1/2 fluid ounce = 15 mL

2 tablespoons = 1/8 cup = 1 fluid ounce = 30 mL

4 tablespoons = 1/4 cup = 2 fluid ounces = 60 mL

5 1/3 tablespoons = 1/3 cup = 3 fluid ounces = 80 mL

8 tablespoons = 1/2 cup = 4 fluid ounces = 120 mL

10 2/3 tablespoons = 2/3 cup = 5 fluid ounces = 160 mL

12 tablespoons = 3/4 cup = 6 fluid ounces = 180 mL

16 tablespoons = 1 cup = 8 fluid ounces = 240 mL

INDEX

NOW THAT YOU'RE COOKING WITH KELLY MINTER, STUDY WITH HER, TOO!

FINDING GOD FAITHFUL
8 sessions

Trace the path of Joseph's life in the Book of Genesis to observe how God's sovereignty reigns, even in our darkest moments.

LifeWay.com/ FindingGodFaithful

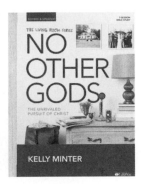

NO OTHER GODS
8 sessions

Learn to identify the functional gods you may unknowingly be serving to experience the abundant life only Jesus can give.

LifeWay.com/NoOtherGods

ALL THINGS NEW
8 sessions

Study the Letter of 2 Corinthians to discover how God can use you no matter your situation.

LifeWay.com/AllThingsNew

WHAT LOVE IS
7 sessions

Dig deep into the Letters of 1, 2 & 3 John to discover not only the heart of John but the heart of Jesus.

LifeWay.com/WhatLoveIs

NEHEMIAH
7 sessions

Look closely at the biblical figure and Book of Nehemiah to allow God to break your heart for a hurting, lost world.

LifeWay.com/Nehemiah

RUTH
6 sessions

Focus on the virtuous character and Book of Ruth to take comfort in her grief and struggles and watch as God rewards her faith and obedience.

LifeWay.com/Ruth